T0305388

Emancipation Through Emotion Regulation at Work

To all born and yet-to-be-born children, in the hope that this book becomes the precursor for a better – emotionally freer – human condition

Emancipation Through Emotion Regulation at Work

Dirk Lindebaum

Cardiff Business School, Cardiff University, UK

Edward Elgar
PUBLISHING

Cheltenham, UK • Northampton, MA, USA

Published by
Edward Elgar Publishing Limited
The Lypiatts
15 Lansdown Road
Cheltenham
Glos GL50 2JA
UK

Edward Elgar Publishing, Inc.
William Pratt House
9 Dewey Court
Northampton
Massachusetts 01060
USA

A catalogue record for this book
is available from the British Library

Library of Congress Control Number: 2016962558

This book is available electronically in the **Elgar**online
Business subject collection
DOI 10.4337/9781786436337

ISBN 978 1 78643 632 0 (cased)
ISBN 978 1 78643 633 7 (eBook)

Typeset by Servis Filmsetting Ltd, Stockport, Cheshire
Printed and bound by CPI Group (UK) Ltd, Croydon, CR0 4YY

Contents

Author biography

Being a carpenter by first profession, holding degrees in civil engineering and construction project management, and having completed his PhD in Organisational Psychology at Manchester Business School, Dirk Lindebaum enjoyed a serpentine career development before he was appointed Professor in Management and Organisation at Cardiff Business School. In keeping with the serpentine tradition, he developed a wider curiosity for diverse notions, constructs, methods and controversies. This appetence for learning and searching led him to pursue a significant body of research around emotions at work, the latest culmination of which you are holding in your hands. In addition, his interest in emancipation has also led him to engage in the burgeoning field of organizational neuroscience, where emancipation refers to the liberation from repressive scientific discourses and technologies which have dehumanizing consequences for workers. Read more about his work at dirklindebaum.eu.

Preface

Until very recently, the mere thought of writing a sole-authored book stirred quite a sense of trepidation in me – double the amount of trepidation because it is the first one too. Seriously, how on earth am I to populate over a hundred pages all by myself if the aim is the conceptual development of a fresh line of thinking? An empirical project would necessitate the inclusion of a method and findings section, so a fair share of the book's volume would be already occupied – by default so to speak. But a purely conceptually driven project? 'A sure recipe to tie myself into (conceptual) knots', I told myself. 'Madness! Don't touch with a barge pole', the inner monologue continued.

But you are holding this book in your hands now, and hopefully will actually be motivated to read it – and still more hopefully will feel it was worth your while doing so. So what happened? There is a fairly simple and undramatic response to that question: for one thing, I was not ready to undertake such a major conceptual task before. Writing a scholarly monograph represents, after all, one of the ultimate intellectual challenges a scholar can undertake. Delving deeply into the literature, while not neglecting a healthy sense of breadth, requires the skill of keeping the 'red threat' for the reader clearly illuminated over numerous pages – which is a somewhat weightier challenge compared to a standard 40-page, double-spaced and strictly margined academic article. For another, I needed to have an idea that would spark both my imagination and determination to pursue this book. It would be presumptuous to state that there was a flash of insight to the extent that the whole argument and structure of the book would lay open before my eyes, literally out of the blue. Far from it. On reflection, I can see that this book represents only the latest and logical extension of a stream of research I have been developing or have been involved in with dear colleagues from my very first publication up to this present moment, and probably for some time to come. But this train of thought fails to convey the struggle involved in writing previous articles or essays in terms of building a persuasive argument – let alone the frustration of having (a fair amount of) submitted manuscripts rejected. It too belies the fact that I was unaware of what – at a more visceral level – actually motivated me to write *what* I wrote, and probably *how* and *why* so too at the beginning of my academic existence. Imagine writing an academic article and being quite aware of the intellectual message or contribution of your work. The article gets published in a journal, and since it is your 'first' publication, chances are you will not forget the moment you opened your email inbox to read the editor's acceptance letter. And yet, only years later, when I started to dwell on the ideas behind this book, I had something that comes close to an epiphany; an emancipatory motivation already shines through in that first publication (Lindebaum, 2009). How can workers be protected against organizational incursions to appropriate their emotions for organizational ends and purposes? How can we safeguard the emotional autonomy of workers in an era when organizations want the hearts and souls of workers? In what ways, and under what conditions, can we attempt to liberate workers from repressive social norms and practices that function *because* of emotion? These questions, taken together, inspired the motif of 'chains' on the cover of this book as a signifier for repressive social norms and practices to metaphorically represent a chained life.

Unfortunately, during my doctoral studies as an organizational psychologist, I was unaware that there was a whole theoretical tradition around emancipation (as chiefly espoused by critical theory) that could have so usefully informed my research. But the engagement with critical theory became a game-changer me for. While there is a multitude of arguments that would be worth mentioning, one of the more salient ones having a catalytic effect upon my work was Connerton's (1976) observation that the strength of power relations in society is due to the fact that these relations 'have not been seen through' (p. 19). It is easy to intellectually process this statement and somehow concur with it. Practically, however, it can be quite a challenge given that many individuals have to work to make a living. Even if workers 'see things through', they may have no choice but to collude in practices that are of a repressive nature to them – when they are under pressure, for instance, to sustain a family. And we should not forget – whether we like it or not – that the need to belong constitutes a basic human need. Thus, the prospect of not belonging any more to a valued organization or social group can be too painful a contemplation for some individuals to endure, so that they prefer dwelling in a 'chained' existence. And yet, this pertains exactly to the quintessence of this book, namely, to raise the reader's awareness that 'the cure for the pain is in the pain' – to borrow from the great Sufi Rumi (1207–1273). It is this unflinching approach, I suggest, that will start breaking up successively each link of the chain until the very last link is entirely liberated – in other words, until the last link of the chain has emancipated itself.

Having pored over myriad books and articles on emotion and related topics surely helped in this respect, but there were also real-life situations that profoundly impacted on me as an individual and academic. Above all, one situation on board a flight in which the cabin crew blatantly abused their power to intimidate a fellow passenger (and later me too) sparked my interest in more differenti-ated approaches to the study of anger, especially what we have since defined as 'moral anger' (Lindebaum and Geddes, 2016). I mention this episode to emphasize that there is a history behind this book that has a strong bearing on its motivation and development.[1]

I guess I am now better able to see these power relations through myself. But make no mistake; I do have my occasional lapses in between. Still, compared to the 'original' state, I feel better off in the state of affairs. These are not vain or trivial observations; in quite significant ways, they help explain why I came to write this book. But just how does one write a book about emotions at work? For the empiricist or rationalist, the probable choice is to write in a disinterested, value-free and objective style, emphasizing the role of *logos* in the articulation of scientific ideas preferably in the distant third person. Within this world-view, this is entirely consistent and appropriate. However, I have developed an ever-greater appetence for normative theories in recent years, and have come to terms with *pathos* as the preference to engage in academic writing as a neces-sary antidote to these bloodless schools of value-free reality.[2] As a result, the book represents an attempt at 'passionate scholarship' (Courpasson, 2013), where real-world and first-hand experiences (as indicated in the Appendix) feed into theoretical pursuits that have political and social relevance – and vice versa.

While the context in which I develop the theorizing is decidedly management focused, the relevance of the ideas presented here is also of importance to the more general readership. Since social relationships are infused with emotions, I do hope that readers will also make connections to other spheres of social life, be they in the context of wider emotion discourses within society or as close as home in the context of families and friends.

Finally, since my aim in this book, in a way, is to provide a recipe and the ingredients for worker emancipation, I am mindful that perhaps I simultaneously provide a recipe and the ingredients for management and organizations to abuse these ideas to strengthen control over the emotions and behaviours of workers. Woe betide any organization that opts for this. May all the curses of the world descend upon it.

NOTES

1. For background and further explanation, please refer to the Appendix, which features a developmental conference paper that my wife and I wrote in response to the dreadful experience.
2. I underline that this is a personal choice I am happy to exercise when the scope of project permits it, but that does not imply that I will bury my head in the sand and cease to collaborate with other colleagues on interesting projects. It simply means that collaborations require – more often than not – compromises to find the common ground among authors.

REFERENCES

Connerton, P. (ed.) (1976). *Critical Sociology*. Harmondsworth, UK: Penguin.
Courpasson, D. (2013). On the erosion of 'passionate scholarship'. *Organization Studies*, **34**(9), 1243–1249.
Lindebaum, D. (2009). Rhetoric or remedy? A critique on developing emotional intelligence. *Academy of Management Learning and Education*, **8**(2), 225–237.
Lindebaum, D., and Geddes, D. (2016). The place and role of (moral) anger in organizational behavior studies. *Journal of Organizational Behavior*, **37**(5), 738–757.

Acknowledgements

With the book completed, I sense a profound amount of gratitude toward a number of exceptional individuals who generously lent their time and experience to its development at varying stages of maturity. To begin with, special thanks go to Robin Holt for having organized a book-writing workshop in Liverpool in December 2014. This event provided an opportune 'deadline' to serve as an incentive to organize the ideas behind the book a little more systematically. During the event, both he and Jean Clarke probed thoroughly the basic rationale and arguments behind this book, which forced me in quite productive ways to continue thinking about its aim and scope. With the proposal ready for submission some time later, Yiannis Gabriel kindly shared his impressive expertise to provide further invaluable feedback. *Euxaristw para polu file mou!* Following the signing of the contract, and as the first drafts of the chapters neared completion, my colleague Deanna Geddes applied her sharp intellect as writer and editor to the text. I am indebted to her for having so generously provided her time and feedback in the refining of the arguments. I also wish to express my gratitude for allowing me to use her Dual Threshold Model of Anger in this book. The permission to Figure 3.1 by Guilford Press and James Gross is also gratefully acknowledged.

To the members of the Cardiff Organisation Research Group (CORGies) at Cardiff Business School, I also express my gratitude for listening to the ideas presented here, and for sharing their thoughtful responses to them at a moment when I was I finalizing the finer nuances of the overall argument of this book.

To Francine O'Sullivan, the editor at Edward Elgar, I would also like to extend my sincere appreciation for her responsiveness and guidance before and throughout the project. For the excellent copy-editing service provided, Michaela Doyle and Maria Anson also deserve thorough mentioning. It was a delight working with them on the book.

Serendipity is such a wonderful feature of human life, and it was exactly through this that I met Guy Farrow on a train journey from Cardiff to Manchester. During the journey, he boarded the train some time later and took a seat across the desk from me. He then opened his rucksack, took out his drawing materials and started to sketch amazing comic sequences. Being in need of a tailor-made book cover, I struck up a conversation about his skills and experience. That was a conversation to behold, for two hours later he came up with the broader idea of the book cover that you can see now. So, to you as well Guy, thanks so much for the inspiration and dedicated approach to completing the cover. If anyone is interested in enlisting his work as illustrator, please do get in touch with him (victoryart@ rocketmail.com). I surely was impressed by his creativity and skill in producing the book cover.

The video animation accompanying this book (to be found on my website, dirklindebaum.eu) was skilfully produced by Nadine Weston, and I would like to extend my thanks to her as well. She can be contacted at http://nadineweston.com.

A very special thank you goes to my favourite and staunchest critic (and wife), Effi, for remaining patient with me throughout the writing of the book and for tolerating my taste for working desks, while always being available for 'quick' consultations when our pathways crossed in the kitchen to prepare a cup of coffee. And finally, to the boys, thank you so much for making it meaningful to get up in the morning and relentlessly work on the issues discussed in this book.

1. Introduction

An attempt to combine the conceptual premises of critical theory and emotion regulation may not appear to be an obvious choice, less so a compatible one for the dogmatic purist. After all, many readers will contend that critical theory and emotion regulation are largely embedded in sociological or psychological thought and history, respectively. This distinction goes beyond disciplinary boundaries; it is, rather, indicative of disparate ontological and epistemological assumptions about the world, as a comparison between key studies in each domain readily reveals (cf. Alvesson and Willmott, 1992; Denny and Ochsner, 2014; Gross, 1998; Horkheimer, 1937/76). And yet, the combination of these traditions, and an exploration of the intellectual space between them, is what I attempt to explore in this book.

No matter how theoretically and practically exciting this exploration might be, it does come at a likely cost; there will be necessarily some scholars protesting that each domain – in its own right – has not received the prerequisite depth and scope to fully cover all angles of the extant literatures. I beg to differ from that criticism, since an all-encompassing treatment of the literature invariably implies traversing the same ground again, when in fact the exploration of the intellectual space between critical theory and emotion regulation offers – so I hope – fresh and stimulating ideas. Acknowledging that this reflects a more pragmatic approach, my aim in this book is to advocate the idea of *emancipating emotion at work* by enabling workers to regulate their emotions *differently* toward that end vis-à-vis the emotional repression they experience at work. In terms of emancipation, many critical theorists argue that it is one key intention of critical theory (Connerton, 1976; Geuss, 1981).

While I scrutinize the key constructs in much more detail in Chapter 2, in the spirit of greater conceptual clarity, it is important to offer a preliminary sketch of how I shall apply the terms 'emancipation' and 'emotion regulation' in this book. To begin with, 'to emancipate' (from the Latin *emancipatus*) refers to a setting 'free from control', or declaring '(someone) free', or to 'give up one's authority over', often in the context of parental control according to the *Online Etymological Dictionary*. Consistent with this, Alvesson and Willmott (1992) define emancipation as 'the process through which individuals and groups become freed from repressive social . . . conditions, in particular those that place socially unnecessary restrictions upon the development and articulation of human consciousness' (p. 432).[1] Throughout this book I shall insist that 'emotion' constitutes a prominent tool of *repressive social control* in terms of how workers both experience and express it.[2] It requires some groundwork to explain this idea in a way that is necessary and appropriate for an introductory chapter, so I hope readers will bear with me on the following pages.

By using critical theory as a guiding framework toward greater worker emancipation, I aim to move forward the conversation around the 'so what?' of emotion in the context of work. That is, it is only when we begin to think about how we talk about and regulate emotion at different levels of analysis within organizations that we can ask *why* and *how* emotion represents a tool of repressive social control. This is a pivotal question, as different levels of analysis (e.g., 'management' or the 'organization' versus the individual worker) entail different goals and different interpretations of outcomes, especially but not limited to the context of emotion research (Lindebaum and Jordan, 2012, 2014).

To explicate this point, consider the possibility of being shamed into better performance at work by co-workers or management placing a cabbage on your desk every Friday if you fail to meet your financial targets. As reported in the news, this practice was employed by managers at two HBOS branches in Scotland (BBC, 2005; but see also Fineman, 2003). Likewise, shame – or, more specifically, the avoidance thereof – is used in Japanese business settings to encourage extra effort and performance in managers. What we can see here is that some organizations aim for enhanced worker performance by using shame as a tool of social repression, while the failing worker incurs psychological suffering, for instance depression (see Martin et al., 2006). Thus, the same emotion generates different outcomes depending on the level of analysis considered.

But how exactly does this example (more are to follow for all emotions of interest here) constitute an act of emotional repression?

For this to be answered, we need to understand what the social function of shame is (both at work and in society). Felt shame is related to negative self-evaluations based upon actual or anticipated depreciation of valued others due to a violation of standards (Creed et al., 2014). From the social functional perspective, shame motivates behaviours that centre on dealing with endangered 'positive' self-views (de Hooge et al., 2010), often in the form of approach behaviours (e.g., reparative actions following one's violation of moral standards). Sometimes, it may be that we have transgressed important moral principles held dear by co-workers. As a result, we can experience shame as self-accusation, and perhaps open up to offer a confession or apology to restore a damaged personal relationship with someone close to us (Solomon, 1993). However, shame can also (and more perfidiously) be employed by management or the organization to endanger one's 'positive' self-view simply because one has not met performance targets at work, as the cabbage example illustrates. Behind this is the motivation (implicit or explicit) to 'teach' workers to be fearful of that shaming experience recurring. It is, therefore, evident that shame is one key emotion to maintaining social control. As Scheff (1990, p. 75) notes, we experience social control as 'so compelling because of emotions', especially the prospect of 'punishment' in the form of, for instance, being publicly shamed.

Because being regularly shamed by others incurs psychological suffering for the shamed 'failing worker' in the form of depression, an ability to regulate emotions differently to avoid this suffering from depression is an initial step of utmost practical importance. This becomes clearer once we consider how emotion regulation is defined, namely as 'the processes by which *individuals influence* which emotions they have, when they have them, and how they experience and express these emotions' (Gross, 1998, p. 275; italics added).[3] But it would be unfortunate to assume that emotion regulation represents one monolithic psychological mechanism. It is vital to remain mindful of the fact that there are several distinguishable emotional regulation strategies (and associated sub-tactics) that have significant bearings upon this book.

While I further detail the relevant sub-tactics in Chapter 3, suffice it to say that, at a broader level, Gross (1998) distinguishes between antecedent-focused and response-focused emotion regulation. These two sets of regulatory strategies can be differentiated by the temporal point at which they primarily (but not exclusively) affect how an emotion is generated. For instance, antecedent-focused strategies occur before a complete emotion and its associated patterns of cognitive, physiological and behavioural responding are induced. By contrast, response-focused regulation strategies are induced once an emotion has been experienced and the associated cognitive, physiological and behavioural responses have been completely generated. These two strategies are worth noting at this stage as they differentially inform subsequent theorizing presented in this book, especially in how they and (some of) their distinct sub-tactics apply to the specific emotions of interest here. I will revisit these strategies in Chapter 3, where their relevance becomes more evident in relation to each emotion examined in this book and how each of these emotions relates to the two pathways to emotional control depicted in Chapter 2.

In relation to the cabbage example and the experience of shame, the definition of emotion regulation stated above implies exercising a degree of choice in influencing whether or not workers follow the appraisal pattern associated with shame detailed above (i.e., negative self-evaluations based upon actual or anticipated depreciation of valued others due to a violation of standards).[4] Since belongingness constitutes a basic human need (Gagné and Deci, 2005), the powerful effect of being shamed in this way is immediately evident.

Being able to regulate one's emotions differently at work – as a result of better understanding its underlying processes – can then be enlisted as a guide toward an emancipated life. Key here is (and I shall revisit this point later) that the attribution of blame for the ostensibly failed performance is negated and that the accused worker understands the difference between shame elicited by legitimate blame – e.g., if he/she has violated a significant moral standard, such as the racist juror in *12 Angry Men* see Lindebaum and Gabriel, 2016) – and shame elicited by purely artificial and external situations (i.e., illegitimate and maladaptive shame) that serves the interests of management by instilling fear not to underperform again at work. In other words, emotion regulation becomes the vehicle through which critical theory affords both an emancipatory quest away from and a close scrutiny of the repressive qualities of emotion when they are abused as tools of social control.

I shall argue that management scholars and others deprive themselves, both theoretically and practically, of considerable opportunity by ignoring what critical theory (with its inherent aim of emancipation) can bring to the literature on emotion regulation, and vice versa. In a way, it is rather fascinating to note, from a more pragmatic perspective, that critical theory and the literature on emotion regulation have enjoyed such an enduring blind spot for each other. If there is under-explored potential for each tradition to inform each other, what, then, are the theoretical and practical arguments to support this claim?[5]

In terms of what emotion regulation can meaningfully add to the notion of emancipation, I wish to advance the thesis that remaining within the traditional confines of critical theorizing implies, by necessity, a lack of progress toward the emancipation of workers in contemporary workplaces relying so heavily on emotion as a repressive tool (or vehicle of social control). By remaining within the traditional confines of critical theorizing, I mean an over-appreciation of structural and relational concerns relegating workers largely to a life of passivity and paucity of agentic impulses (Geuss, 1981; Marcuse, 1968/2009). I would go further still by arguing that the notion of emancipation and the conceptualization of workers as passive pieces in a larger jigsaw of social relations are fundamentally at variance. In my view, the evidence demonstrating the capacity of individuals to act in agentic, self-efficacious and self-determining ways provides sufficient justification to underline this internal inconsistency. For instance, while Bandura (2000, p. 75) admits that we 'are partly the products of [our] environments', he adds that 'by selecting, creating, and transforming [our] environmental circumstances, [we] are producers of environments as well. This agentic capability enables [us] to influence the course of events and to take a hand in shaping [our] lives'.[6]

However, it would be incomplete to suggest that only emotion regulation illuminates a hitherto underexposed angle in the theorizing around emancipation. I speculate here that we can gain a better and deeper understanding of emotion regulation if we were to appreciate emancipation as one (but not exclusive) moral endpoint as to *why* we regulate our emotions. This would appear plausible, since the ultimate end of emancipation is to enable individuals in society to modify their lives by nurturing in them a sense of understanding and self-knowledge of their social conditions which can then function as the foundation for such modification (Fay, 1987).

However, on the surface, one might insist that the ability to regulate emotion adaptively presents a mere psychological buffer to protect workers from undue emotional strain and expectations at work. After all, to simply regulate emotions differently so as to limit the impact of the emotional event on the worker will not necessarily change that which imposes these emotional strains and expectations – e.g., service jobs requiring the display of a happy face (see Grandey et al., 2015; Hülsheger and Schewe, 2011). In fact, one might go further to argue that it might even be ethically imperative to foster that kind of better emotion regulation ability among affected workers. As an initial step, I am sympathetic to this contention, for in doing so workers can start working toward greater emotional emancipation at work. In the longer term, however, the viability of this perspective starts to disintegrate once we endeavour to ascertain the normative endpoints that guide and orient why we regulate emotion a priori.[7] As Charland (2011) observes, 'the "how" and the means of emotion regulation always logically presuppose certain ends, which in the final instance prescribe "why" emotions should be regulated *one way rather than another*' (p. 84; italics added). With a keen eye on this why consideration, the question then becomes this: given those working conditions which impose the emotional strain upon workers, why would they voluntarily and continually cooperate in their own repression? Why should they – in the long run – regulate their emotions in one way (the detrimental one) rather than another (the beneficial one) to adopt the question raised by Charland above? The point I wish to convey is that, although workers cannot always quit their jobs due to a variety of reasons (sustaining one's life or that of one's family is surely a most pressing one), after prolonged exposure to emotional pressure there will be at some point the irresistible desire to change one's situation, which in itself is already a way to regulate one's emotions – i.e., by selecting another situation which is less emotionally draining (see Gross, 1998).[8] In light of this, the theoretical utility of applying the aims of critical theory to the field of emotion regulation manifests itself. Critical theory does this by providing the end to which emotion regulation might be applied; that is, workers' emancipation from repressive emotional conditions.

However, if critical theory wishes to remain faithful to its aim to emancipate, it must relax its conceptual faithfulness to social ontologies, for otherwise it remains a fancy intellectual edifice with reduced practical relevance and potential. Likewise, if psychologists are serious about emotion regulation as a predictor of health outcomes (Davidson et al., 2007; Denny and Ochsner, 2014; Gross and John,

2003; Gross and Muñoz, 1995), they must engage more with socio-logical issues, such as socio-emotional norms and work patterns, as causes of ill-health (see Mason, 2015, for recent first-hand accounts of this). This has only been recently insinuated (Gross, 2013), but requires much more careful consideration of the normative elements reflected in critical theory.

1.1 THEORETICAL AND PRACTICAL RELEVANCE

To better understand the theoretical and practical relevance of this book, it is useful to briefly elaborate further upon the intersections between the literatures on emancipation and emotion regulation. For instance, Geuss (1981) states that a successful critical theory reflects a transition from an initial state of delusion, bondage and frustration (hereafter referred to generally as 'suffering') to a final state of knowledge, freedom and satisfaction (hereafter referred to generally as 'liberation'). He continues that a typical critical theory comprises three elements, succinctly summarized as:

1. an element showing that the transition between the initial and final state is *theoretically possible*;
2. an element highlighting that the transition between the initial and final state is *practically necessary*; and
3. an element asserting that the transition between the initial and final state is feasible only *if the worker subscribes fully* to the idea of emancipation as espoused by critical theory.

In relation to the aim and scope of this book, this entails that emotion regulation can serve as the psychological construct to help accomplish the transition between the initial and final state when that which is repressive is emotion. That is, this focus shows that it is *theoretically possible* to complete that transition. In addition, the suffering of workers in response to emotional strains at work renders it *practically necessary* to advocate the idea of emancipating emotion through regulating emotions differently in order to alleviate emotional suffering (see also Mumby and Putnam, 1992). By emotional suffering, I mean the adverse psychological and physiological consequences that workers experience at work as a result of emotion constituting sophisticated vehicles of repression and social control. In so positing, I note that the adverse psychological and physiological consequences are not exclusively caused by the imperative to engage in 'emotional labour' and the associated suppression of emotion, which will be the presumptive 'prime suspect' for many readers. In Chapter 2, I expand further upon this. Finally, it requires the presence of workers who embrace the need for greater emancipation as a result of emotional repression at work.

In terms of timing, the initiation of this book project is not a whimsical or random act. Instead, synthesizing the disparate intellectual domains of critical theory and emotion regulation in the context of management studies *now* is germane for several reasons. First, I shall insist that there are emotional mechanisms now at play that constitute the very repressive social conditions that critical theory is typically concerned with. In addition to the cabbage example stated earlier, it has been known for some time that employees' displays of 'friendly demeanours' are related to job descriptions and consequent rewards (i.e., wages). However, it is well documented that engaging in emotional labour (Hochschild, 1983), which requires workers to regulate their emotions according to the display rules imposed by organizations, can have detrimental consequences for them, such as the experience of burn-out and exhaustion (Grandey et al., 2015; Hülsheger and Schewe, 2011). However, a more recent and more ominous development is that failure to display such friendly demeanours entails that the entire shift in a fast-food restaurant might lose out on its bonus (as opposed to a single worker being reprimanded by management for failing to be 'happy' at work). Just because one worker was seen as 'grumpy', all co-workers would be punished (Mason, 2015), implying that the grumpy worker is likely to experience or is being subjected to intense emotional pressure (e.g., being faced by angry colleagues and the fear that might entail). Although this contemporary work example is testament to the highly repressive conditions that emerge when emotions constitute tools of control, prior studies on 'concertive control' offer similar arguments (e.g., Barker, 1993).

However, at the time critical theory was first articulated, and over intervening years, emotion research across disciplines and including critical theory was barely seeing the light of day.[9] Indeed, the notion of emotional labour was not even given intellectual birth yet at that time (i.e., being first articulated in 1983 by Hochschild). Instead, original and subsequent critical theorists exhibited a keen focus on reason and rationality through which the emancipated state of being can be achieved (Geuss, 1981; Marcuse, 1968/2009; but see also Alvesson and Willmott, 1992). Of note, critical theorists like Horkheimer and Adorno struggled with the limitations of human reasons as drivers of emancipation, while they were aware of them (see Alvesson and Willmott, 1992).

Since emancipation is not a given, but involves an oftentimes painful struggle as workers negotiate more internal emotional processes (e.g., fear of being excluded) and external behavioural expectations (e.g., behaviour geared toward social acceptance), the exploration of emancipation through the lens of emotion regulation may hold important theoretical and practical insights for management research. Indeed, it appears rather curious that the role of emotion (and associated processes) does not feature more explicitly in the exegeses of critical theory (but see Fay, 1987, for an exception). Further to this, domination – as conceived by more contemporary critical theorists – rests upon, *inter alia*, the internalization of norms (with its implicit 'emotive' content) and emotional control (Murray and Ozanne, 2006). Further still, exploring the topic in the context of work is highly germane as we spend most of our waking hours during the day at work. In this respect, I have argued before that the expression of emotions is progressively cast into a simplified mould, reflecting the restricted range of those emotions whose display is desired by the organization (Lindebaum, 2012), adding Fineman's (2001) observation that the scale of such organizational interventions is 'grand'. This, in turn, has significant consequences for if and how we can lower our guards to let shine through how we really feel and think at work. I am reminded of the work by Cederström and Fleming (2012), who provocatively argue that 'henceforth, our authenticity is no longer a retreat from the mandatory fakeness of the office, but the very medium through which work squeezes the life out of us' (p. 36).

And finally, as I have already acknowledged in the Preface, it is only after having pored over myriad books and articles that I am now better able to see through how emotions can be enlisted as a means of social control, and the consequences that we experience at the individual level in response to this. But simply being better at this does not mean there are no lapses occurring any more. True to the spirit of critical theory, however, I am comfortable in noting that the current state is concretely more preferable than the original one.

1.2   BOUNDARIES AND CLARIFICATIONS

Like many other ideas or topics before, the theorizing presented in this book is subject to a number of boundary conditions, or requires several points of clarification to delineate its theoretical scope. Appreciating these in the formulation of new ideas is pivotal to ensure that the conditions under which new theoretical ideas are supposed to hold are clearly communicated to the readership. Below I elaborate briefly on:

- the subset of critical theory that inspired this book;
- the scope and limits of emancipation;
- the way I employ the notion of 'normative' here;
- the preliminary range of discrete emotions that qualify as prime suspects for repressive/social control;
- the level of analysis at which I situate this book; and
- the writing style which I shall pursue in this book.

I note that the latter aspect is not a vain or idle addition, but rather a matter of significant theoretical and thought-generative ramification.

1.2.1   Which Subset of Critical Theory?

To begin with, critical theory has been influenced to a significant extent by members of the Frankfurt School. Although critical theory serves as the overarching descriptor, it is erroneous to presume that the critical theorists of that era have produced a monolithic corpus of intellectual heritage. It is neither within the scope of this book nor is it its purpose to contrast these distinctive positions. Interested readers can consult existing introductions on the evolving positions of major contributors within the School (Connerton, 1976; Held, 1980). Likewise, commentators suggest that critical theory lacks definite meaning, as it has been used in many different ways since the heyday of the School (Murray and Ozanne, 2006). Instead, I shall limit myself to exploring the notion of 'criticism' as one form or critique that emerged in the tradition of critical theory.[10]

There are at least three characteristics of criticism that have a strong bearing on the contents that follow. First, it focuses on something particular and concrete, rather than something that is anonymous. Thus, it explicitly recognizes the existence of a subject. Second, this notion of criticism is applied to 'objects of experience whose "objectivity" is called into question; [it] supposes that there is a degree of inbuilt deformity which masquerades as reality' (Connerton, 1976, p. 20). The aim is thus to remove this distortion, thereby permitting the liberation of that which has been distorted. It is for this reason that emancipation is inherently entwined with the notion of criticism and liberation. And third, criticism seeks to change or even remove those conditions of what is often referred to as false consciousness (Geuss, 1981; Marcuse, 1968/2009). In so doing, criticism seeks to render visible that which has been hidden previously. Therefore, it can be the catalyst for critical self-reflection to occur, whether for workers or groups. Throughout this book, when references to critical theory are made, it is this angle of critical theory that should be borne in mind.

1.2.2 Scope and Limitations of Emancipation

As far as the scope and limitations of emancipation are concerned, there are several possible angles to be explored. First, as stated before, for a critical theory to be confirmed it is crucial that workers must agree that their 'former' state was that of suffering (along the lines already defined). Also, the 'present' state must be one of increased (emotional) freedom and satisfaction, coupled with a more accurate view of *the workers'* true interests and needs. So, while critical theory may try to help initiate the laudable goal of emancipation, it cannot be precluded that workers' first taste of emancipation may be too terrifying for them to endure and, consequently, prompt them to conclude that they were better off in their original state (Geuss, 1981). After all, Sartrean thought holds that the burden of autonomy (emotional here) is not light (Alvesson and Willmott, 1992).

There is a second angle to be recognized here: rather than being a gift bestowed upon workers by management, emancipation is not a given, but requires the '(often painful) resistance to, and overcoming of, socially unnecessary restrictions, such as fear of failure' (Alvesson and Willmott, 1992, p. 433). And while it is known that the lack of exposure to painful memories and events deprives individuals from experiencing both intrinsically valuable and important memories that are axiomatic for personal or emotional growth (Lindebaum and Raftopoulou, 2014), the fear of failing en route to emancipation might prevent some workers from accepting the emancipatory invitation in the first place. This comment is not offered lightly at this juncture; earlier critical theorists, such as Erich Fromm, had a keen understanding that it lies in a person's innate nature that he or she does not want to be free. Writing in *Escape from Freedom* (1941), he argued that man wants to be controlled by a higher authority, and will be fearful of freedom.

Third, if workers are happy already at *this moment in time*, they are not a fit subject for a critical theory (Fay, 1987).[11] In all cases, the goal of critical theory to emancipate would be disconfirmed. Therefore, for emancipation to be successful, workers must not be emotionally inhibited (due to fear of failure) to begin with, and must regard the new state of existence as preferable to the original one. What must be crucially borne in mind is that the emancipatory journey does not only represent a formidable struggle for the worker. Instead, unrestricted emancipation and free thinking stands in often stark contrast to present knowledge about effective and productive organizing (Alvesson and Willmott, 1992). If this assumption is correct, how then might dissatisfaction with the status quo prompt workers to alter their conditions both within and in relation to social structures? I will revisit this question later in Chapters 3 and 4.

As a further point of clarification, the way I enlist the term 'emancipation' should not be confused with the perhaps deceptive notion of existential liberation, where workers are encouraged to seek 'opportunities for the fulfillment of their needs' (Alvesson and Willmott, 1992, p. 433) – for as long as this fulfilment coexists with desirable organizational consequences such as performance. Likewise, it should not be confounded with the notion of neo-normative control, where individuals seemingly have a choice to 'be themselves' and 'have fun' at work. This newer incarnation of normative control is often disguised as individual empowerment and freedom, which, in the end, are nothing but subtler ways of controlling individuals at work by way of 'capturing their sociality, energy and "authentic" or "non-work" personalities as emotional labour' (Fleming and Sturdy, 2011, p. 177). Instead, emancipation, as advocated here, aims to provide deeper insights into how emotions can be regulated differently in order to generate radical or assertive worker action (cf. the case of anger in social movement studies – Jasper, 1998). It is a process – in the form of more adaptively regulating one's emotions – that starts internally and unfolds through the sense-making processes of the workers (rather than being imposed or advocated externally by consultants and researchers, as in the case of 'empowerment').

Seen in this light, and bearing in mind how emotion regulation has been defined earlier, once workers understand the pathological nature of emotion repression (and how it is enlisted at work to make them behave in narrowly defined ways), they can potentially morph into 'emotional deviants'; that is, those workers who fail or refuse to obey emotion norms. Consequently, they are often stigmatized and subjected to social controls (such as being shamed into conformity) even though, under some conditions, they can become agents of social change (Thoits, 2004).

1.2.3   How 'Normative' is Applied

Critical theory reflects normative aspirations; it combines empirical analysis (i.e., what is) with normative theorizing (what ought to be). The normative connotation of critical theory is most concisely expressed by Durkheim (1893/2014), who notes that only 'because what we propose to study is above all reality, it does not follow that we should give up the idea of improving it' (p. 4). Naturally enough, the very notion of normative theorizing is likely to prompt objections from empiricists or rationalists, who entertain the assumption of an 'objective distance between research and practice and who believe that their research is largely free of political and moral assumptions' (Suddaby, 2014, p. 2). But even considering how the notion of 'normative' is being played out among critical theorists themselves deserves scrutiny.

Let us consider, for instance, the argument that critical theory (being normative in kind) 'claims to inform [individuals] about what interests it is rational for them to have' (Geuss, 1981, p. 58). I argue that this thinking reflects another internal inconsistency of critical theory. With reference to facts, I can well relay to the reader what the current science says in relation to how emotion can serve as a tool of social control (and the consequent costs for workers). However, if I wanted to cast my theorizing consistent with recent works on normative theories in management studies, it is central to explicitly recognize that there are natural limits in our role as social scientists in completing the emancipatory journey of others. We can initiate it but much less ought we to complete it, for this would run counter to the very notion of emancipation advocated here.

To elaborate: simply raising the awareness that the present repressive (emotional) condition for workers is unhealthy *for* them is very different from then prescribing *to* them what they should feel as a result of experiencing emancipation. The problem is this: we need to develop greater awareness of what 'normative' implies. My contention is that, as indicated previously, if normative is construed from the perspectives of researchers, then true emancipation may remain a laudable yet unfulfilled condition. To borrow from Suddaby (2014), theory can serve various ends, and normative theory may offer its own genre of theoretical claims, including examples where normative elements (such as perceptions of right and wrong and resultant action) form part of a construct's definition. The key distinguishing feature of normative theories is that perceptions of right and wrong are reserved for actors based upon their ethical values, rather than pre-imposed by researchers (for a detailed theoretical example on 'moral anger', see Lindebaum and Geddes, 2016).[12]

Put differently, it seems imperative that we create space for workers to interpret the consequences of an initiated or ongoing emancipation through their own sense-making and life histories. I argue that both the challenge and opportunity to approach critical theory with renewed vigour is to be explicit in appreciating the ethics and values of employees at work as an engine that constructs reality rather than as a camera that captures it (MacKenzie, 2006). This has important consequences for critical theorists, for it illustrates the limits of their involvement in initiating, accompanying and concluding the emancipatory journey of workers. In the context of this book, I shall claim that the involvement of a critical theorist must be limited to the initial phase or, more exactly, to provide the catalyst inducing the kind of critical insights from which emancipation can then blossom. Although I am sympathetic to the ideas of some critical theorists, I am not convinced that there is sufficient differentiation in terms of these different stages in extant critical theorizing. For instance, Fay (1987, pp. 82–3) argues that:

> Critical social science arises out of, and speaks to, situations of social unhappiness, a situation which it interprets as the result both of the

ignorance of these experiencing these feelings and of their domination by others. It is this experience of unhappiness which is the wedge a critical theory uses to justify its entrance into the lives of those it seeks to enlighten and emancipate.

I agree *in principle* with the intentions raised by Fay, but I also point out that it does not indicate whether the critical theorist is supposed to conclude the emancipatory journey of repressed workers. Therefore, by placing the values and ethics of workers centre stage, we must exercise caution in professing to be able to exactly predict what kind of consequences that initial critical insight might entail for them. Therefore, the way I conceive emancipation here, and this is how I see emancipation providing the 'moral endpoint' (i.e., the *why*) of emotion regulation, is to raise awareness among workers that current emotional demands at work (e.g., whether a result of emotional labour or peer pressure) are to their detriment – psychologically, physically and socially. To raise this awareness is, in my view, the task of a critical theory. However, the 'ought to' frequently invoked as the normative element in critical theory can entice researchers to go beyond this initial yet fundamentally crucial step and advocate *what* workers should *do* as a result of these insights.

I disagree with this temptation, for it is presumptuous on the part of researchers to prescribe to workers what they should be doing as a consequence of having gained the insight that the emotional demands placed upon them are excessive. Consistent with this approach, I have refrained from offering precise predictions in terms of what workers might experience along their emancipatory journey, or indeed what the final 'phenomenological' outcome of it might be (though I admit to offering some speculations in terms of the latter in relation to structural changes). What I have done instead is to argue that insights gained along the emancipatory journey will lower the likelihood that workers experience the raft of adverse psychological, physiological and social consequences that they would experience had they not had these insights. This is very different from positing that either X or Z will be the consequence – in the phenomenological sense – of the emancipatory journey. As highlighted later in Chapter 4, what this approach permits is for the phenomenological world of workers to be shaken up, stirred or unsettled in order to settle thereafter in a new (and more advantageous) way.

Further to this, any prediction or advice in relation to the exact outcomes of worker emancipation from emotional repression would seem to be diametrically opposed to the frequently invoked notion within critical theory of workers having the potential and need for creative, spontaneous and autonomous action (Alvesson and Willmott, 1992; Grandey et al., 2015). Instead, I advocate the position that the effects of emotion research more generally, and its effects in the context of this book, often do not immediately manifest themselves. Instead, they rather develop over time as the insights are applied to, or judged against, current or even future real-life situations. It is then the iterative and cumulative interaction between the insights offered in this book and how workers continuously apply these to *their own* life histories and situations that will create an 'impact' over time. Consequently, it is key to how we make sense of all this; and it is noteworthy that emotions are intimately entwined with our sense-making processes because emotions both initiate and are the outcomes of sense-making (Dougherty and Drumheller, 2006).

1.2.4   Range of Emotion Examined

Emotion researchers have produced numerous lists of emotions (see e.g., Kleinginna and Kleinginna, 1981; Lazarus and Cohen-Charash, 2001). It should be understood, however, that some emotions are more theoretically relevant than others in the context of this book. In consequence, I have based the inclusion of particular emotions upon their theoretical relevance to the articulation of the two pathways to social control as characterized in Chapter 2. To avoid distraction from the main arguments here, I only very briefly foreshadow these characteristics. Key for the pathways to social control is the literature on the social functions of emotions (Keltner and Haidt, 1999; Keltner and Kring, 1998; Lench et al., 2015), and it is in this light that I discuss the emotions of particular interest in this book – namely, shame, guilt, happiness and anger. While Pathway I relies upon an excessive exploitation of the social function of emotion (as I propose is the case with shame, guilt and happiness), Pathway II indicates that the 'talk about emotions' overrides its social function (as is the case with anger). Crucially, vis-à-vis the multi-dimensional nature of emotion regulation (as indicated above and further elaborated upon in Chapter 3), the various strategies (and associated sub-tactics) we can use to regulate emotion at work and beyond do not apply indiscriminately across both pathways.

In Chapter 2, I define each of the aforementioned emotions and illustrate both their relevance to the theorizing around these pathways and the ambition to initiate the emancipatory journey of workers. Since this book marks a fresh starting point in the debate, I am in no way insinuating that the theorizing presented here might not apply directly to other emotions as well. It may well, but since I wrote this book with a view to opening up the conversation around emancipating emotions – as opposed to settling or containing the issue – I hope that the reader is receptive as to why these initial choices had to be made from a theoretical point of view.[13]

Further to this, I understand that, unlike the primary focus on the four emotions identified, there is a case to be made for a secondary focus on how these emotions can lead to the experiences of other emotions, such as fear, further down the appraisal process. For instance, recent studies suggest that individual reactions to the experience of shame (elicited by negative evaluations by valued others) tend to correlate with the fear of negative evaluations – i.e., the fear we might experience in relation to negative evaluations (see Yoon, 2015). In addition, prior research has shown that the experience of shame can itself generate feelings of other-directed anger and hostility. For instance, studies have shown that an acute sense of shame can induce a sense of 'humiliated fury' directed towards the self and towards real or imagined disapproving others (Tangney et al., 1996). Because shame implies the perception of exposure to and disapproval from others, self-directed hostility is readily directed towards others who are part of the shame-eliciting event.

Lastly, given the range of so-called discrete emotions circulating in the literature (Lazarus and Cohen-Charash, 2001), broadening the range of emotions included would, I maintain, dilute the theoretical focus of this book. However, I find ample motivation here for future research on the topic by considering whether and/or how the theorizing presented here can be applied to other emotions as well – either in the primary or secondary sense detailed above – and I hope that other researchers also perceive this motivation to further engage with these ideas. Note that, for each emotion under investigation, I have written a vignette to underline the practical necessity of this book. Some characters were inspired by conversations I had with friends or colleagues in relation to their prior experiences (i.e., 'John' and his experience with shame or 'Thomas' and his anger episode in a hospital ward). In the case of guilt-prone 'Jennifer', I took inspiration from the relevant literature to come up with a realistic scenario. Doing so also enabled me to adhere theoretically to the definition of guilt and how it relates to other constructs. I have also examined the content of widely used questionnaires to inform the vignettes. Lastly, several newspaper articles (especially Noah, 2013 and Resnikoff, 2013) served as inspiration in developing the character of 'Maria' and her constant need to appear radiant when serving customers in a food outlet. Taken together, I am confident that these vignettes have representational character and breathe live into the theorizing presented in this book.

1.2.5   Levels of Analysis

The theorizing I present here is situated – in the first place – at the within-person level of analysis, even though these effects are often initiated by social cues consistent with the focus on social functional accounts of emotions (Keltner and Haidt, 1999). To elaborate on these social cues, emotions signal behavioural intentions of others to us (Van Kleef, 2014), while others add that 'interpersonal factors are essential in emotion regulation, because emotion regulation develops within a social context and continue to include social relations throughout life' (Hofmann et al., 2016, p. 342). As an indication of just how much social context influences the frequency of emotion regulation in everyday life, Gross and colleagues (2006) have shown that, within a sample of 91 young adults, 98 per cent of emotion regulation episodes took place in the presence of other people (each participant was asked to recall one such episode during the past two weeks).

Despite the prevalence of social cues, it is at the within-person level of analysis that I propose the theoretical and practical parameters presented in this book are being played out as a result of the self-efficacious or agentic capacities of workers identified. More precisely, I am interested in how the theorizing presented in this book affects the dynamic fluctuations in workers' experience and expression of emotions, and their consequences (Ashkanasy, 2003). This is different from the ubiquitous focus among work psychologists on between-person variance (or individual differences in terms of cognitive abilities or personalities). For some scholars steeped in critical management studies more generally, and in emancipation more specifically, this focus may represent a theoretical inconsistency. After all, critical management studies – and the specific reference therein to emancipation – adhere to more structural, social or institutional ontologies (Alvesson and Willmott, 1992; Geuss, 1981; Murray and Ozanne, 2006).

Critical theorists have been vocal in maintaining that, while changes in the individual's (or agent's) attitudes or beliefs may be sufficient in the psychoanalytical sense, they cannot be the final ambition of critical theory. Reflecting on the work of Habermas, Geuss (1981) argues that 'if coercive institutions of the society are intact, it is not enough for the oppressed agents to have gained an inner freedom from compulsion to believe in their legitimacy' (p. 86). And yet, while I agree that structural/institutional changes ought to be the long-term goal of an emancipation that moves beyond the worker, the undue and persistent disregard for the possibility of agentic self-transformation and how the emancipatory process can unfold among workers within workplaces and society to form a larger 'critical mass' has, I propose, often rendered the emancipatory potential of critical theory impotent. This circumstance is regrettable, both theoretically and practically, because an undue faithfulness to dogmatic purity in the context of critical theory (in its own right and as applied to management studies) undermines that which it sets out to achieve (i.e., emancipation from repressive social conditions). While I will delve into greater detail later, workers' capacity not only for self-transformation, but also for acting in defiance of social structures with a view to changing them is borne out, for instance, by the literature on emotional deviance. For instance, it suggests that:

> because individuals are not totally determined by the structures or cultures in which they live, but can exercise agency, creativity, and autonomy, they may, in unjust or oppressive circumstances, redefine their deviant feelings as valid and proceed to use these new normative understandings to persuade others to pursue social change. (Thoits, 2004, p. 374)

That social change or innovation can take many shapes and forms, such as new value norms and behaviours, as Thoits furthermore underlines. As I shall elaborate later, in the context of emotion research (in management studies and beyond), there is an intimate link between self-determination and the engineering of self-fulfilling prophecies (see e.g., Solomon, 2003).

1.2.6 Writing Style

Since critical theory provides one main source of inspiration for this book, and since the examination of this book's aim necessitates a more unorthodox approach, I have adopted essayistic prose here. In describing the characteristics of essays, Adorno and colleagues (1954/84, p. 171) were quite clear that 'the law of the innermost form of the essay is heresy. By transgressing the orthodoxy of thought, something becomes visible in the object which it is orthodoxy's secret purpose to keep invisible'. Therefore, through normative reflections on and challenges to existing conditions, the essay enables us to sketch how the world might be. But this may necessitate a departure from what Habermas (1987) referred to as 'scientism', or science's belief in itself, which reflects the conviction that we cannot grasp science as one form of possible knowledge, but must instead identify knowledge with science.

The essay permits reintroducing reflection and spontaneous insights and can, therefore, aid in the generation of new thinking in management and beyond (Delbridge et al., 2016). Taken further still, the essay constitutes an *intervention* both in terms of academic debates influencing political debates (see Gabriel, 2016) and in terms of actually making a difference to the readers' professional and private lives. In some quirky way, this book represents a 'counter-intervention' to the interventionist sentiment in the West that we have to exercise a degree of control over our emotions (Gross, 1998; Mayer et al., 2000). With this counter-interventionist intention in mind, it is surely my hope that – in one form or another – this will crystallize over time. For the purpose of this book, this intervention is characterized by the use of reprise, a rhetorical device typical to critical thought implying a continual return to a motif or problem to prise open its aspects. For Adorno, the 'technique of reprise was necessary to a mode of presentation aimed at filling-out of meanings; and it was by such indirections that he did not so much impart an achieved knowledge but enacted the processes by which insights are *earned*'(Connerton, 1976, p. 14; italics added). This goes straight to the aim of this book to squarely identify that which causes emotional suffering, without being too prescriptive about what consequences workers may aspire to as a result of these insights being earned.

In sum, and to be very clear, I contend that the arguments presented above do in no way invalidate the theorizing attempted here; they are simply an honest recognition of the limits of generalizability that affects a good deal of management research (Dubin, 1976; Johns, 2006).

1.3   CHAPTER OVERVIEW

The remainder of this book evolves along the following lines. In Chapter 2, I shall prise open in more detail how the social functions of emotion in itself, or deviations from them, can be co-opted to serve as a means of social control. To do so, I start by defining emotion consistent both with the key construct emotion regulation (as scrutinized in more detail in Chapter 3) and the notion of emancipation as featured in the critical theory literature. Second, I briefly touch upon the literature on the functions of emotion, and how these manifest themselves across levels of analysis. Third, I introduce the reader to the central arguments in this book appertaining to Pathways I and II and their purpose as tools of social control. The motivation is to show how the social functions of emotion (or a divergence from them) can be enlisted to serve as a means of social control. Fourth, having explicated and unpacked how these pathways operate, I then join these insights with the literature on critical theory to maintain that the social functions of emotion (or, again, deviations from them) constitute a sophisticated system of repression, the seeing through of which can potentially spark within repressed workers a desire to emancipate themselves from these conditions.

With the pathways to social control articulated, it is then opportune to examine more closely in Chapter 3 the theoretical parameters and the empirical findings associated with the emotion regulation literature. This leads me to offer first a general overview of the emotion regulation literature, including important and germane technicalities associated with Gross and Thompson's (2007) process model of emotion regulation. These include:

- the role of appraisals;
- the scope of goals implicated in the emotion regulation process;
- the role of context and feedback loops;
- the difference between intrinsic and extrinsic regulation; and
- whether emotion regulation represents conscious and/or unconscious processes.

Because it is within the theoretical and empirical parameters of emotion regulation studies that I locate one potential catalyst to initiate the emancipatory journey of workers, it then becomes necessary to offer a more detailed examination of the strategies available to regulate emotion (i.e., antecedent- vs. response-focused emotion regulation strategies, and their various sub-tactics). Having laid this groundwork, it is then possible to join distinct emotion regulation tactics with the pathways to social control in order to show a potential avenue from a repressed to an emancipated existence of workers. More specifically, I provide a flowchart to indicate – for each pathway – the probable appraisals that currently entail adverse psychological, physiological and social consequences for workers (Figure 3.2). The flowchart then moves on to propose how these adverse consequences can be circumvented by way of appraising the emotion-eliciting event differently (i.e., either through reappraisal or the genuine expression of emotion). With this in mind, I propose that the preceding step can then create 'new consequences' for workers. Importantly, and consistent with my reservation to predict what these consequences are exactly in the phenomenological world of workers, I suggest that there will be a reduced likelihood that adverse psychological, physiological and social consequences for workers will actually occur.

It is necessary at this juncture to highlight in advance a distinctive feature in that flowchart. Even though the logic behind both pathways remains intact, when it comes to appraising situations differently, happiness branches out from Pathway I and points jointly with anger (Pathway II) to the genuine expression of emotion. Chapter 3 provides the theoretical rationale for doing so. In Chapter 4, the final chapter, I shall offer a synthesis of the main arguments developed throughout this book. This synthesis leads me to propose another flowchart (Figure 4.1), which illustrates the key premises and stages of the emancipatory journey of workers. That is, it illustrates the process from social control via regulating emotions differently now towards an emancipated existence of workers in the future. Note that Figure 4.1 does not represent a 'model' in the hypothetico-deductive sense, setting out propositions for empirical testing. Instead, it should be considered as an organizing framework to synthesize the contents of the preceding chapters.

NOTES

1. The preceding connotations represent, however, a passive voice (i.e., someone *else* as the active agent is doing something to you). So it is worth noting that the same dictionary also contains a reference to making 'his or her own way in the world'. The difference here between the active and the passive voice is not merely an issue of semantics; it goes straight to the core of the theorizing I attempt to develop in this book – that is, who initiates, accompanies and concludes the emancipatory journey of workers. I will revisit this point later in the book.
2. This thought has enjoyed a prominent place in sociological studies for some time (Scheff, 1988, 1990), but it is also increasingly appreciated in management studies (Fineman, 2001; Learmonth and Humphreys, 2011; Lindebaum, 2012; Lindebaum and Ashkanasy, forthcoming; Murphy and Kiffin-Petersen, 2016).
3. The italics in the quote serve to underline the active role of workers in the process of regulating their emotions differently toward greater emancipation.
4. I offer this argument as strictly applicable to the shaming of individuals in response to failed expectations at work. Needless to say, I emphasize the important function of felt shame in response to moral standard violations when it induces reparative actions following violations of moral standards. The powerful effect of shame is lucidly illustrated in the movie *12 Angry Men*, when – in a highly dramatic move – 11 jurors turn their backs on the 12th juror following his racial slurs (Lindebaum and Gabriel, 2016).
5. Pertinently, Gross (2013, p. 363) argues that 'a more complete understanding of the causes and consequences of emotion regulation will be facilitated via cross-fertilization among affective scientists across disciplines', including sociology, business and psychiatry.
6. This observation is offered in the context of studies on self-efficacy (see also Bandura, 1997, for more evidence on this). Bandura defines perceived self-efficacy as being concerned with our belief in our ability to influence events that affect our lives. Further to this, the question of agency vs. structure is one of the perennial puzzles in social sciences research, especially as we look for causal explanations or proofs. I am in no way suggesting that we can *always* exercise individual agency vis-à-vis structural concerns. However, given the evidence indicated above, it is important to appreciate that it is possible to exercise individual agency in some situations. Beyond the evidence already enlisted, there are such notable individuals who defy structural concerns and display highly agentic behaviours. In a recently aired obituary (31 May 2016), the German public broadcaster ARD showed a former interview with Rupert Neudeck, founder of Cap Anamur, a humanitarian organization whose goal is to help refugees and displaced people worldwide. In it he stated that 'we could only do it [i.e., rescue Vietnamese 'boat people' in the late 1970s/early 1980s] by completely ignoring the rules of the world, the rules of bureaucracy, and the rule of governments. Only looking to save humans in danger.' Equipped with this determination and the attitude to ignore rules, his organization saved the lives of more than 10 000 boat people.
7. This 'temporal' argument paves the way for a more detailed treatment in Chapters 3 and 4 of the influence of time in the emancipatory journey of workers.
8. In the remainder of this book, I shall maintain that situation selection comes close to what critical theorists would consider along the lines of 'structural changes' as the ultimate manifestation of worker emancipation.
9. A content analysis of the American Psychological Association's PsycINFO database on 7 June 2016 showed that the keyword 'emotions' featured 2851 times

in publications between 1930 and 1960. This period serves as an appropriate range to include, as many initial and subsequent key writings in critical theory were published then. By contrast, between 1960 and 2016, the keyword appeared 258 922 times in the same database, underscoring thereby the exponential interest in emotions as a scientific subject. I appreciate that these numbers are not organized by specific disciplines, but several reviews underline that this exponential growth also affected the study of emotions in management and the psychological study of emotion regulation (Ashkanasy, 2003; Gross, 2013).

10. The other form/critique is 'reconstruction', which attempts to grasp anonymous systems of rules which can be followed by any subject, provided that the individual possesses the necessary competence (Connerton, 1976).

11. This point must be taken with a pinch of salt, as it cannot be precluded that the workers' 'happiness' is the result of the very veil of delusion of reality that critical theory seeks to lift.

12. There are several examples in the psychological literature where researchers have imposed *their* values on construct definitions, the constructs of emotional intelligence and coping being only two examples (see Gross, 1998; Lindebaum and Jordan, 2014 for critial appraisals on this).

13. Some readers might argue that an alternative lens through which to identify relevant emotions is the widely used, yet deplorably ill-informed, global description of so-called 'negative' (or positive) emotions and the associated notion of 'valence', a term borrowed from physics and chemistry (see Solomon, 2003). Solomon explains at some length that the positive–negative polarity (or the idea of 'emotional' opposites) has its genesis in ethics, and not in the scientific study of emotions. I argue that these descriptions are unfortunate at best, and at worst lead to inaccurate theorizing (and bad management practice). Partly as a result of this, I maintain that it is more expedient both theoretically and practically to focus on the utility of a discrete emotion as it relates to context (Lindebaum and Jordan, 2012, 2014), hence my preoccupation with functional account of emotions.

REFERENCES

Adorno, T. W., Hullot-Kentor, B., and Will, F. (1954/84). The essay as form. *New German Critique*, **32**(Spring–Summer), 151–171.

Alvesson, M., and Willmott, H. (1992). On the idea of emancipation in management and organization studies. *Academy of Management Review*, **17**(3), 432–464.

Ashkanasy, N. M. (2003). Emotions in organizations: a multi-level perspective. In F. Dansereau and F. J. Yammarino (eds), *Multi-Level Issues in Organizational Behaviour and Strategy* (Vol. 2, pp. 9–54). Oxford: Elsevier.

Bandura, A. (1997). *Self-Efficacy: The Exercise of Control*. New York: Freeman.

Bandura, A. (2000). Exercise of human agency through collective efficacy. *Current Directions in Psychological Science*, **9**(3), 75–78.

Barker, J. R. (1993). Tightening the iron cage: concertive control in self-managing teams. *Administrative Science Quarterly*, **38**(3), 408–437.

BBC (2005). Cabbage dig causes furrowed brows. Retreived from http://news. bbc.co.uk/1/hi/scotland/4155334.stm (16 August) on 12 January 2010.

Cederström, C., and Fleming, P. (2012). *Dead Man Working*. Alresford, UK: Zero Books.

Charland, L. C. (2011). Moral undertow and the passions: two challenges for contemporary emotion regulation. *Emotion Review*, **3**(1), 83–91.

Connerton, P. (ed.) (1976). *Critical Sociology*. Harmondsworth, UK: Penguin.

Creed, W. E. D., Hudson, B. A., Okhuysen, G. A., and Smith-Crowe, K. (2014). Swimming in a sea of shame: incorporating emotion into explanations of institutional reproduction and change. *Academy of Management Review*, **39**(3), 275–301.

Davidson, R. J., Fox, A., and Kalin, N. H. (2007). Neural bases of emotion regulation in nonhuman primates and humans. In J. J. Gross (ed.), *Handbook of Emotion Regulation* (pp. 47–68). New York: Guilford Press.

de Hooge, I. E., Zeelenberg, M., and Breugelmans, S. M. (2010). A functionalist account of shame-induced behaviour. *Cognition and Emotion*, **25**(5), 939–946.

Delbridge, R., Suddaby, R., and Harley, B. (2016). Introducing JMSSays. *Journal of Management Studies*, **53**(2), 238–243.

Denny, B. T., and Ochsner, K. N. (2014). Behavioral effects of longitudinal training in cognitive reappraisal. *Emotion*, **14**(2), 425–433.

Dougherty, D. S., and Drumheller, K. (2006). Sensemaking and emotions in organizations: accounting for emotions in a rational(ized) context. *Communication Studies*, **57**(2), 215–238.

Dubin, R. (1976). Theory building in applied areas. In M. D. Dunnette (ed.), *Handbook of Industrial and Organizational Psychology* (pp. 17–39). Chicago: Rand McNally.

Durkheim, E. (1893/2014). *The Division of Labor in Society*. New York: Free Press.

Fay, B. (1987). *Critical Social Science*. Cambridge, UK: Polity Press.

Fineman, S. (2001). Emotions and organizational control. In R. Payne and C. L. Cooper (eds), *Emotions at Work: Theory, Research and Applications for Management* (pp. 219–240). Chichester: Wiley.

Fineman, S. (2003). *Understanding Emotion at Work*. London: Sage.

Fleming, P., and Sturdy, A. (2011). 'Being yourself' in the electronic sweatshop: new forms of normative control. *Human Relations*, **64**, 177–200.

Fromm, E. (1941/2011). *Escape from Freedom*. New York: Ishi Press.

Gabriel, Y. (2016). The essay as an endangered species: should we care? *Journal of Management Studies*, **53**(2), 244–249.

Gagné, M., and Deci, E. L. (2005). Self-determination theory and work motivation. *Journal of Organizational Behavior*, **26**(4), 331–362.

Geuss, R. (1981). *The Idea of a Critical Theory: Habermas and the Frankfurt School*. Cambridge: Cambridge University Press.

Grandey, A. A., Rupp, D., and Brice, W. N. (2015). Emotional labor threatens decent work: a proposal to eradicate emotional display rules. *Journal of Organizational Behavior*, **36**(6), 770–785.

Gross, J. J. (1998). The emerging field of emotion regulation: an integrative review. *Review of General Psychology*, **2**(3), 271–299.

Gross, J. J. (2013). Emotion regulation: taking stock and moving forward. *Emotion*, **13**(3), 359–365.

Gross, J. J., and John, O. P. (2003). Individual differences in two emotion regulation processes: implications for affect, relationships, and well-being. *Journal of Personality and Social Psychology*, **85**(2), 348–362.

Gross, J. J., and Muñoz, R. F. (1995). Emotion regulation and mental health. *Clinical Psychology: Science and Practice*, **2**(2), 151–164.

Gross, J. J., Richards, J. M., and John, O. P. (2006). Emotion regulation in everyday life. In D. K. Snyder, J. A. Simpson, and J. N. Hughes (eds), *Emotion Regulation in Families: Pathways to Dysfunction and Health* (pp. 13–35). Washington, DC: American Psychological Association.

Gross, J. J., and Thompson, R. D. (2007). Emotion regulation: conceptual foundations. In J. Gross (ed.), *Handbook of Emotion Regulation* (pp. 3–24). New York: Guilford Press.

Habermas, J. (1987). *Knowledge and Human Interest*. Cambridge: Polity press.

Held, D. (1980). *Introduction to Critical Theory*. London: Hutchinson.

Hochschild, A. R. (1983). *The Managed Heart: Commercialization of Human Feeling*. Berkeley: University of California Press.

Hofmann, S. G., Carpenter, J. K., and Curtiss, J. (2016). Interpersonal Emotion Regulation Questionnaire (IERQ): scale development and psychometric characteristics. *Cognitive Therapy and Research*, **40**(3), 341–356.

Horkheimer, M. (1937/76). Traditional and critical theory. In P. Connerton (ed.), *Critical Sociology* (pp. 206–224). Harmondsworth, UK: Penguin.

Hülsheger, U. R., and Schewe, A. F. (2011). On the costs and benefits of emotional labor: a meta-analysis of three decades of research. *Journal of Occupational Health Psychology*, **16**(3), 361–389.

Jasper, J. M. (1998). The emotions of protest: affective and reactive emotions in and around social movements. *Sociological Forum*, **13**(3), 397–424.

Johns, G. (2006). The essential impact of context on organizational behavior. *Academy of Management Review*, **31**(2), 386–408.

Keltner, D., and Haidt, J. (1999). Social functions of emotions at four levels of analysis. *Cognition and Emotion*, **13**(5), 505–521.

Keltner, D., and Kring, A. M. (1998). Emotion, social function, and psychopathology. *Review of General Psychology*, **2**, 320–342.

Kleinginna, P. R., and Kleinginna, A. M. (1981). A categorized list of emotion definitions with suggestions for a consensual definition. *Motivation and Emotion*, **5**, 345–379.

Lazarus, R. S., and Cohen-Charash, Y. (2001). Discrete emotions in organizational life. In R. Payne and C. Cooper (eds), *Emotions at Work: Theory, Research and Applications for Management* (pp. 45–84). Chichester: Wiley.

Learmonth, M., and Humphreys, M. (2011). Blind spots in Dutton, Roberts and Bednar's 'Pathways for positive identity construction at work': 'You've got to accentuate the positive, eliminate the negative'. *Academy of Management Review*, **36**(2), 424–427.

Lench, H. C., Bench, S. W., Darbor, K. E., and Moore, M. (2015). A functionalist manifesto: goal-related emotions from an evolutionary perspective. *Emotion Review*, **7**(1), 90–98.

Lindebaum, D. (2012). I rebel – therefore we exist: emotional standardization in organizations and the emotionally intelligent individual. *Journal of Management Inquiry*, **21**(3), 262–277.

Lindebaum, D., and Ashkanasy, N. (2017). A 'new' heart for institutions? Some elaborations on Voronov and Weber. *Academy of Management Review*, forthcoming.

Lindebaum, D., and Gabriel, Y. (2016). Anger and organization studies: from social disorder to moral order. *Organization Studies*, **37**(7), 903–918.

Lindebaum, D., and Geddes, D. (2016). The place and role of (moral) anger in organizational behavior studies. *Journal of Organizational Behavior*, **37**(5), 738–757.

Lindebaum, D., and Jordan, P. J. (2012). Positive emotions, negative emotions, or utility of discrete emotions? *Journal of Organizational Behavior*, **33**(7), 1027–1030.

Lindebaum, D., and Jordan, P J. (2014). When it can be good to feel bad and bad to feel good: exploring asymmetries in workplace emotional outcomes. *Human Relations*, **67**(9), 1037–1050.

Lindebaum, D., and Raftopoulou, C. E. (2014). What would John Stuart Mill say? A utilitarian perspective on contemporary neuroscience debates in leadership. *Journal of Business Ethics*. doi:10.1007/s10551-014-2247-z.

MacKenzie, D. (2006). *An Engine, Not a Camera: How Financial Models Shape Markets*. Cambridge, MA: MIT Press.

Marcuse, H. (1968/2009). *Negations: Essays in Critical Theory*. London: MayFly Books.

Martin, Y., Gilbert, P., and McEwan, K. (2006). The relation of entrapment, shame and guilt to depression, in carers of people with dementia. *Aging and Mental Health*, **10**, 101–106.

Mason, P. (2015). Politicians love dressing up in hi-vis vests, but they ignore what's really happening to modern workers. *The Guardian*, 12 April.

Mayer, J. D., Salovey, P., and Caruso, D. R. (2000). Models of emotional intelligence. In R. J. Sternberg (ed.), *Handbook of Human Intelligence* (2nd edn, pp. 396–420). New York: Cambridge University Press.

Mumby, D. K., and Putnam, L. L. (1992). The politics of emotion: a feminist reading of bounded rationality. *Academy of Management Review*, **17**(3), 465–486.

Murphy, S. A., and Kiffin-Petersen, S. (2016). The exposed self: a multilevel model of shame and ethical behavior. *Journal of Business Ethics*, 1–19. doi: 10.1007/s10551-016-3185-8.

Murray, J. B., and Ozanne, J. L. (2006). Rethinking the critical imagination. In R. W. Belk (ed.), *Handbook of Qualitative Research Methods in Marketing* (pp. 46–58). Cheltenham, UK and Northampton, MA, USA: Edward Elgar Publishing.

Noah, T. (2013). Labor of love: the enforced happiness of Pret A Manger. *New Republic*. Retrieved from https://newrepublic.com/article/112204/pret-manger-when-corporations-enforce-happiness on 12 June 2016.

Resnikoff, N. (2013). How companies force 'emotional labor' on low-wage workers. Retrieved from www.msnbc.com/the-ed-show/how-companies-force-emotional-labor-low on 12 July 2016.

Scheff, T. J. (1988). Shame and conformity: the deference-emotion system. *American Sociological Review*, **53**(3), 395–406.

Scheff, T. J. (1990). *Microsociology*. Chicago: University of Chicago Press.

Solomon, R. (1993). *The Passions: Emotions and the Meaning of Life*. Indianapolis: Hackett.

Solomon, R. (2003). *Not Passion's Slave: Emotions and Choice*. Oxford: Oxford University Press.

Suddaby, R. (2014). Editor's comments: why theory? *Academy of Management Review*, **39**(4), 407–411.

Tangney, J. P., Wagner, P. E., Hill-Barlow, D., Marschall, D. E., and Gramzow, R. (1996). Relation of shame and guilt to constructive versus destructive responses to anger across the lifespan. *Journal of Personality and Social Psychology*, **70**(4), 797–809.

Thoits, P. A. (2004). Emotion norms, emotion work, and social order. In A. S. R. Manstead, N. Frijda, and A. H. Fischer (eds), *Feelings and Emotions: The Amsterdam Symposium* (pp. 357–376). Cambridge: Cambridge University Press.

Van Kleef, G. A. (2014). Understanding the positive and negative effects of emotional expressions in organizations: EASI does it. *Human Relations*, **67**(9), 1145–1164.

Yoon, H. J. (2015). Humor effects in shame-inducing health issue advertising: the moderating effects of fear of negative evaluation. *Journal of Advertising*, **44**(2), 126–139.

2. Emotion, its function and emancipation from social control

In this chapter, I aim to lay bare in more detail how the social functions of emotion (or a divergence from them) can be co-opted to serve as a means of social control. To this end, I first define emotion in this book in a way that is both consistent with the key construct emotion regulation (as scrutinized in more detail in Chapter 3) and the notion of emancipation as espoused by critical theory. Second, I briefly review the literature on the functions of emotion and how these manifest themselves across levels of analysis. Next, I introduce two pathways to social control to show how the social functions of emotions (or a divergence from them) can be enlisted to serve as a means of social control. Having made visible how these pathways operate, I then connect these insights to the literature on critical theory to argue that the social functions of emotions (or, again, a divergence from them) constitute a sophisticated system of repression, the seeing through of which can spark within repressed workers a desire to emancipate themselves from these conditions.

2.1 DEFINING EMOTIONS

In this chapter, I shall elaborate upon how and why the emotions of particular interest in this book (i.e., shame, guilt, happiness and anger) can serve as tools of social control. Toward this end, it is necessary to first define the term 'emotion' in a manner that is both consistent with the definition of emotion regulation offered in the introduction (see Suddaby, 2010, for an elaboration on construct clarity) and with the overall attempt to theoretically explore the notion of emancipation as initiated by different approaches to regulating emotions at work.

At an abstract level, emotion conveys meaning about relationships (Schwarz and Clore, 1983), most notably when something of significance to us is at stake. On some occasions, an emotion is practically elicited automatically, such as when we recoil in fear from a threatening situation (a bear charging at us in the woods). On other occasions, an emotion is only elicited after considerable appraisal of the situation at hand (Frijda, 1986), such as when we experience shame following a transgression of moral standards. The former scenario is consistent with Zajonc's (1980, 1984) insistence that emotions can exist independent of cognition, while the latter speaks to Lazarus's (1984) claim that cognitions necessarily must precede emotion. Either way, Gross (1998) argues that emotion generates a coordinated set of behavioural, experiential and physiological response tendencies which, in combination, impinge upon how we react to perceived environmental opportunities and challenges.[1]

In retaining a close conceptual adherence to emotion regulation as defined earlier, I subscribe to Solomon's (1993) conceptualization of emotions. Reading his work has, over the years, proffered an affluent fountain of inspiration and reflection about how I approach the study of emotion. In departing from the demeaning view of emotions as distractions or intrusions (see Young, 1936, for a rather extreme view), Solomon insisted that 'emotions are judgments' and constitute 'ways of seeing and engaging' with the world, our ways of 'being tuned' into the world (pp. viii–ix). He continues by suggesting a further key characteristic of emotion; he confronts head on the myth of passions as a self-serving myth, dramatized for the purpose of our own self-image in the form of the myth of passivity: 'the self-serving half-truth is the fact that we often *suffer* from our passions, submit ourselves to them, find ourselves carried away, and foolishly behaving because of them' (Solomon, 1993, p. xv; italics added). But, Solomon cautions, for as long as this passive view of emotions prevails, the most significant and crucial attitudes and actions of our lives are outside the scope of our responsibilities and doing. Accordingly, he reasons, we place ourselves in a convenient and sophisticated web of excuses. Rejecting the idea that emotion passively imposes itself upon us, Solomon argues that every emotion is a strategy, 'a purposive attempt to structure our world in such a way as to maximize our sense of personal dignity and self-esteem (p. xviii), including the usual disclaimer when it comes to 'strategies'.[2]

In a later work, Solomon (2003) developed the above arguments further to explicitly denote emotion as individual 'choices' and, therefore, individual 'responsibilities'. This marks another sharp departure from the perspective of emotions as occurrences that passively afflict us. Indeed, Solomon is circumspect in outlining his emotions-as-choice perspective, admitting that emotions are often non-deliberate 'choices'. But he offers intriguing insights as to how we can bring these choices more to the conscious forefront. For instance, he admits that we cannot simply produce or have an emotion; nor can we readily stop having one in the first place. He insists, however, that we can open ourselves up to persuasion, argument and evidence:

> We can force ourselves to be self-reflective, to make just those judgments regarding the causes and purposes of our emotions, and also to make the judgment that we are all the while choosing our emotions . . . In a sense, our thesis here is self-confirming: *to think of our emotions as chosen is to make them our choices* [italics added]. Emotional control is not learning to employ rational techniques to force into submission a brutal 'it' which has victimized us but rather the willingness to become self-aware, to search out, and to challenge the normative judgments embedded in every emotional response. To come to believe that one has this power *is* [italics in original] to have this power. (Solomon, 2003, p. 17)

Even though Solomon is renowned, *inter alia*, for his philosophical accounts of emotion, it is noteworthy that his perspective on emotion as representing individual choices and strategies is consonant with the volitional character of emotion regulation as articulated by Gross (1998) in the first chapter.[3] Having clarified how emotion is conceptualized, in the next section I will succinctly review the key characteristics of functional accounts of emotion.

2.2 FUNCTIONS OF EMOTIONS ACROSS LEVELS OF ANALYSIS

More generally, functions are recognized in aetiological accounts of the genesis and development of a behaviour, trait or system (Wright, 1973). Functions, thus conceived, 'refer to the history of a behaviour, trait, or system, as well as its *regular* consequences that benefit the organism, or . . . the system in which the trait, behaviour, or system is contained' (Keltner and Gross, 1999, p. 469; italics added). More specifically, functional accounts differentiate discrete emotions in relation to consequences of goal-directed behaviour, and assert that they solve problems important to social relationships and ongoing interactions (Keltner and Gross, 1999). The social functional perspective suggests that responses linked to 'each discrete emotion are theorized to address the adaptive problem that gave rise to that emotion' (Lench et al., 2015, p. 91). Applied, for instance, to the study of anger, this implies that redressing injustice is both a function and a consequence of anger. To illustrate, this approach was recently applied to 'moral anger', defined as:

> (i) an aroused emotional state stemming from (ii) a primary appraisal of a moral standard violation that (iii) impacts others more than oneself, and (iv) prompts corrective behavior intended to improve the social condition, even in the face of significant personal risk. (Lindebaum and Geddes, 2016b, p. 743).[4]

Functional accounts of emotion span also the whole range of levels of analysis. Consistent with the identification of the within-person level of analysis as the key focus at which the theorizing presented here is situated, scholars suggest that the functions of emotion can serve the individual to respond to different adaptive problems – such as the facilitation of physiological, perceptual and cognitive processes – which allow the individual to respond adaptively to significant challenges or opportunities in their environment (Keltner and Gross, 1999). Further to this, the functions of emotion play out at the social or inter-organismic level of analysis. Of note, this interactional level constitutes the focal level of emotions at work (Ashkanasy, 2003). In this context, emotion informs us about the behavioural intentions of others, provides clues as to whether we approach or avoid a situation, and scripts our social behaviour according to prevailing situational constraints (Gross, 1998; Thoits, 2004). When motivated by moral concerns, emotion also serves the function to suppress selfishness and facilitate cooperation with others (Haidt, 2008). Here, it manifests itself that emotions have strong social and, therefore, relational connotations.

Another level of analysis centres on the organizational- and societal-level functions of emotions. It does so by addressing the way in which emotions can benefit larger social groups and organizations (Lutz and White, 1986). In other words, emotions such as anger help organize internal processes, guide social interactions and influence organizational policies (Geddes and Callister, 2007; Lindebaum and Geddes,

2016b). While I recognize that other scholars have proposed a slightly different taxonomy of levels of analysis within management/organizational behaviour (OB) research (Ashkanasy, 2003), for the sake of a parsimonious presentation, I will refrain from a much refined treatment of all these levels of analysis. Due to theoretical expediency, I will focus instead on the within-person level of analysis as the locus of agency, while I want to explicitly state that these internal processes are often initiated by social cues (e.g., being shamed/humiliated by management or peers for poor performance at work).[5]

2.3   FUNCTIONS AS SOCIAL CONTROL AND ITS LINK TO EMANCIPATION

In this chapter, I posit that social functional accounts of emotion offer a fascinating glimpse into the possibilities of emotion as a tool of social control. This may appear counterintuitive, since functions are thought to *regularly benefit* us after all, as indicated earlier. However, I contend that social functional accounts of emotion offer at least two pathways to social control hitherto largely unrecognized by management scholars (for an embryonic exception, see Lindebaum and Jordan, 2014).

But before I delve into these pathways in more detail, and at the risk of stating the obvious, it may be worth recalling that, where there is control, power tends to lurk in its shadow. What frequently links power and control, in turn, is emotion. Carl Rogers, in his book *On Personal Power*, outlines this nexus with incredible acumen, stating that the word 'politics' has acquired a new set of meanings in contemporary psychological and social usage. That is, it concerns power and control. More elaborately put, politics concerns:

the extent to which persons desire, attempt to obtain, possess, share, or surrender power and control over others and/or themselves. It has to do with *the maneuvers, the strategies and tactics, witting or unwitting*, by which such power and control over one's life and others' lives is sought and gained – or shared or relinquished. It has to do with the *locus of the decision-making power* [italics in original]: *who makes the decisions, which, consciously or unconsciously, regulate or control the thoughts, feelings, or behavior of others or oneself* [italics added]. It has to do with the effects of these decisions and these strategies, whether proceeding from an individual or a group. (Rogers, 1977, pp. 4–5)[6]

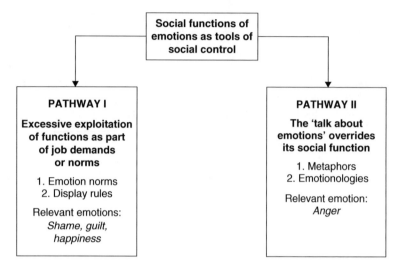

*Figure 2.1   Social functions as means to emotional control at work:
the two pathways*

In responding to the question who makes the decisions that regulate
our thoughts and emotions at work, I note that it may be sometimes possible to pinpoint individuals or groups. However, more
generally, it is also a useful starting point to explore through what
mechanisms this regulation occurs (bearing in mind that these are,
or course, human made). Thus, I shall propose here two distinct
pathways to social control, as illustrated in Figure 2.1. Importantly,
when hereafter I refer to the social functions of emotion as means of
social control, it must be borne in mind that I either imply that these
functions are stretched in their scope to impose excessive strain on
workers (Pathway I) or that talk about the emotion overrides its very
function (Pathway II).[7]

Throughout this book, I shall underline that these pathways constitute the highly repressive social conditions that I want to enable
readers to 'see through', and thereby help dissolve or at least weaken
them. This is consistent with the view that critical theory should
aspire to contribute to the liberation of workers from 'unnecessarily
restrictive traditions, ideologies, assumptions, power relations, identity formations, and so forth, that inhibit or distort opportunities for
autonomy, clarification of genuine needs and wants, and thus greater
and lasting satisfaction' (Alvesson and Willmott, 1992, p. 435). In

the following section, I unpack the arguments pertaining to each pathway in greater depth.

2.3.1   Pathway I

In terms of Pathway I, I posit that the modern workplace can be an arena in which the 'function' of emotion is excessively used (or even abused). This pathway, I suggest, is specific to emotions of shame, guilt and happiness.[8] These emotions serve as tools of social control *because of* their social functions (i.e., these functions are exploited excessively).[9] For instance, the social function of shame is to signal 'threats to the social bond'; and that 'shame signals a potential threat to survival' if the latter implies belongingness to a group rather than an isolated existence (Scheff, 2003, p. 247). Therefore, sometimes the prospect of being excluded from a social group that one perceives as significant (e.g., a high-flying and successful team at work) is too painful to endure for some workers, so that they can be readily manipulated in such a way that benefits the group (e.g., conformity and compliance with group norms) but is detrimental to them, i.e., negative health consequences (see e.g., Lindebaum, 2009). Accordingly, individuals are motivated to seek approval (the belong-ingness desire) and avoid sanctions (e.g., social exclusion following public shaming), thus hiding or regulating their truly felt emotions in situations where these expectations (or norms) are violated at work. The cabbage example serves to underline this point.

In view of this, despite the function of emotion in social settings, one central argument of the book is that these benefits may wear out if the function is exploited excessively. More specifically, I maintain that two related yet distinct phenomena can potentially pose a risk to social functions of emotion and the consequences they serve for both workers and social groups. These are (i) display rules (Diefendorff et al., 2011) and (ii) emotion norms in society (Thoits, 1989). As indi-cated in Figure 2.1, these phenomena differentially gain prominence in relation to shame, guilt and happiness. To put this more exactly, I explore shame and guilt through the lens of emotion norms as social control mechanisms, while happiness (or a friendly demeanour) is discussed in the context of display rules at work. More details on the rationales for including these emotions are provided later in this chapter.

2.3.1.1   Emotion norms around shame and guilt

Emotion norms are defined as 'beliefs about the appropriate range, intensity, duration, and targets of private feelings in given situations' (Thoits, 1989, p. 322). In the context of work, for some organizations it is seemingly of central concern to own, govern and manipulate the private feelings of their workers for their ends (Cederström and Fleming, 2012; Fineman, 2001, 2003). In addition, while norms can facilitate human interaction, they are also liable to abuse if norm strength and/or content is excessive or dysfunctional, thus rendering them pathological for the worker. This observation is particularly relevant, since individuals tend to seek approval (e.g., pride of belonging to a powerful or popular social group) and avoid sanctions (e.g., fear of being excluded from those groups). For instance, and more generally, Liu and colleagues (2015) report that existing staff and clients socialize newcomers into risky behaviours (such as heavy drinking). The context is such that newcomers observe client behaviour in order to better understand how to best meet job-relevant objectives and expectations. These observations inform performance-related motives, which then prompt the adoption of these risky behaviours that are detrimental to newcomer health as well as effectiveness at the organizational level. More specifically, in the context of emancipation, norms are also key to repressive social conditions (cf. the 'cabbage' example). The 'underperforming' worker's experience of being publicly shamed is likely to lead to an increase in negative physiological and psychological effects such as the release of the stress hormone cortisol and depression (see Dickerson et al., 2004). For the social group (say, a company department), however, the consequence might be that higher performance targets are met and that more revenues are generated – at least in the short run. In the following section, I discuss shame and guilt through the lens of emotion norms.

Shame   Felt shame is related to negative self-evaluations based upon actual or anticipated depreciation of valued others due to a violation of standards (Creed et al., 2014). Previous research defined shame, quite evocatively, as 'sudden, unexpected exposure coupled with blinding inner scrutiny' (Kaufman, 1989, p. 18). Key to understanding shame is that it can leave one feeling exposed to others as defective in some real or perceived way. Importantly, the above references to 'anticipated' or 'perceived' implies, and opens up to debate, the point whether it has an identifiable cause in the classic sense, for much of the emotion may emanate from an inner dialogue that may only loosely relate to a clearly identifiable cause (Kiffin-Petersen and Murphy, 2016). Even though the shame elicitor may initially occur in interactions with co-workers, through internalization an inner monologue can be initiated that, over time, becomes ever more remote from the initial eliciting situation. For instance, a recent study on sick doctors and the obstacles that prevent their return to work found that participants reported a negative response to their situation (i.e., absence from work due to ill health) from co-workers. Over time, these responses were more internalized as opposed to being challenged, and participants referred to terms such as 'failure', 'uncomfortable' and 'shame' when describing themselves (Henderson et al., 2012). Thus, the feeling of being somewhat of a failure morphed into a more general self-perception instead of being specific to the loss of the work role, leading some doctors to conclude that 'there was shame, there was fear . . . there was low self-esteem' (Henderson et al., 2012, p. 6).

In addition to previous observations in this chapter, shame also motivates behaviours that centre on dealing with endangered 'positive' self-views from the social functional perspective (de Hooge et al., 2010), often in the form of approach behaviours (e.g., reparative actions following one's violation of moral standards). In light of this, it is readily apparent how easily (and more perfidiously) shame can be employed to endanger one's 'positive' self-view, simply because one has not met performance targets at work or one fails to conform to the behaviours management or co-workers expect one to display. On a more humorous note (i.e., from the spectator's perspective), this is depicted in the animation movie *Despicable Me*, with the little girl punished by being made to stay in 'the box of shame' for not having sold enough cookies. On a more serious note, I include Vignette 2.1 to show the practical relevance of these arguments.

Consider also the famous conformity experiments by Asch (1956), who aimed at demonstrating the dynamics of conformity in groups. He documented that group pressure compelled individuals toward conformity. The task at hand consisted of stating aloud which comparison line (three different lengths were provided) was identical with the target line, the correct response being obvious. Only one real participant was present (in a group of seven associates of the research team), who sat at the end of the row and gave his/her answer last.

VIGNETTE 2.1: SHAME

Meet John, a married, 35-year-old software engineer and father of two young children. Even though he resides with his family in the UK, he works for a software development firm based in Germany. John is part of a 'virtual' team of five employed to develop tailor-made software solutions for a variety of client needs. A key characteristic of the virtual team, in this case, is that it is self-directed with no formal hierarchy. The assumption is that all potential solutions to problems are openly discussed, and that the team members agree on the exact decisions to be taken.

It follows from this that the senior management of the firm plays hardly any a role in the day-to-day running of the project, except perhaps when things go woefully wrong. More importantly, however, is that any recognition and approval (and sometimes disapproval) is derived from peers only. John uses the analogy of a 'fraternity' to describe the team climate. Hence, peer pressure is the mechanism through which control is exercised. Unless it is prolonged and clearly ascribable to one specific software engineer, it will be the team that takes the blame for any project failure.

For a previous project that ran for about 18 months, John worked with colleagues (all male), who were geographically dispersed, with some residing in the UK, the US and continental Europe. To develop the product according to specification and to deliver it on time requires the team to work closely together over that period. Complexity issues demand that the timeframe is broken down into smaller units, about two to three weeks in duration normally. These periods are called 'sprints' in software jargon, and are part of a software development methodology commonly referred to as 'scrum process'.*

The consequence is such that the team members convene every day via an online platform to discuss three key questions:

- What did each member do yesterday?
- What is each member planning to accomplish today?
- What are the factors obstructing progress?

The questions are designed to ensure that everybody is on the same page as far as product development is concerned. This is vital as all team members simultaneously work on the same document or code every day. As John says emphatically, 'you'll never write on a code alone' if you are part of a virtual team of software engineers. All the more, it is crucial that strict protocols are established to modify the code. If everybody adheres to it, there should be no problems. If, however, one engineer breaches the protocol, then it may undo or interfere with the work of colleagues. 'Never break the build – it's a crime', John repeatedly underlines.

At some point, on having actually disregarded the 'never break the build' rule, a colleague John referred to as the 'process guy' (i.e., the person who keeps everybody in check) introduced what was interchangeably referred to as the 'funny hat' or the 'hat of shame'. It was an accidental introduction of a random hat that happened to lie on the desk next to the computer when the team convened online. It was a 'joke', as John suggested. It was never perceived as vindictive or a top-down imposition (and how could it vis-à-vis a lack of hierarchy in the team?). For the process guy, it was a way of putting his hands up to indicate 'Sorry, my bad call, so I wear the hat now.'

Continuing in the joking spirit, the other team members adopted the notion of the hat of shame, and actually got 'funny' hats themselves in case they broke the build, in order to send an apologetic signal. There was no fuss whatsoever in adopting the hat among the team members. Thus, as a way to remind team members that the integrity of the build is sacrosanct, the hat of shame became institutionalized as a tool to shame colleagues (always under the guise of humour) for their mistakes, which, in turn, would adversely affect the product development for which the entire team was responsible.

The effectiveness of shame as a tool to control the behaviour of the team members was particularly visible in light of the only source of approval and recognition being their peers. The recognition from these 'valued others' thus matters considerably for the software engineers. After all, being shamed generates negative self-evaluations based upon actual depreciation of these valued peers due to a violation of performance standards.

John is still working for the same firm now, but in a different team. But he knows through informal contacts that the 'hat of shame' practice was still in place after he left the previous team. In his current team, John laughs, the hat of shame would be seen as 'juvenile'.**

Notes:
* Scrum is typically regarded as an iterative and incremental agile software development framework for governing the development of a product. It is a holistic approach marked by 'built-in instability, self-organizing project teams, overlapping development phases, "multilearning," subtle control, and organizational transfer of learning' (Takeuchi and Nonaka, 1986, p.137). Combined, these characteristics are said to enable a fast and flexible process for new product development.

** I had several conversations with John (a pseudonym of course). During one conversation, he mentioned 'the hat' in passing. However, this fleeting reference stimulated my curiosity, as I was in the midst of writing the proposal for this book. Having mentioned that I was writing a book upon which his story has direct bearings, John, in turn, asked more questions about how the hat came to serve to control his team's behaviour. He never thought about the hat in a way other than it being a joke, but our conversations prompted him to reconsider this interpretation. It would be presumptuous to suggest that our conversations 'changed everything', but I hope that they at least helped to start 'seeing things through'.

To avoid being visibly different, many individuals (nearly one-third of all cases) succumbed to the conformity pressure to agree with the patently incorrect group consensus.

A subsequent analysis of this experiment by Scheff (1990) associates Asch's findings with the underlying emotional mechanisms. He maintains that the response occasioning the conformity was induced by shame such that 'the fear that they were suffering from a defect and that the study would disclose this defect' (p. 90). It is, therefore, evident that shame is one key emotion to maintaining social order and control. Scheff (1990, p. 75) adds that we experience social control as 'so compelling because of emotions', especially the prospect of 'punishment' in the form of, for instance, shame. Accordingly, in extreme forms, shame plays a key role in the process of social ostracism. Specifically, individuals resisting organizational socialization rituals are sometimes subject to certain disengagement power tactics; they are ignored or ostracized as nonconformists by colleagues or more senior members of staff wishing to enforce compliance (Williams and Sommer, 1997). Consider, for example, the case of a young lawyer who renewed his drinking habit after being ostracized by colleagues for stopping it. Realizing the detrimental consequences of such a habit, he eventually resigned and became a teacher (Frith, 2006).

As I shall outline in Chapter 3, once workers gain a better understanding of how shame can be regulated in *their* favour, given the abuse of its social function, then emancipation is more likely to emerge. In other words, the emancipatory significance of being able to more adaptively regulate the experience and expression of shame resides in the fact that the 'failing employee worker' is less likely to experience the adverse physiological and psychological consequences associated with the experience of shame – such as the release of cortisol and depression (see Dickerson et al., 2004).

Guilt Prior research defines guilt as 'a dysphoric emotion that follows failure to fulfill expectations' (Flynn and Schaumberg, 2012, p. 124). From a social functional perspective and its functional action orientation (Tangney, 1990), guilt-prone individuals tend to feel a sense of urgency in taking corrective action in response to personal failure. If the failure is of a moral or ethical kind (e.g., having lied to a valued friend or co-worker), then the utility of the function of guilt is only too apparent, as corrective action can imply an attempt to offer a sincere apology and thereby restore trust in that relationship. However, consistent with the parameters of Pathway I, the social function of guilt can also be subverted for organizational benefits. Guilt-prone individuals are, as noted earlier, highly motivated to make amends and will exert considerable energy toward this end (Baumeister et al., 1995). If we consider guilt in terms of failure to fulfil performance expectations at work (as opposed to failure to meet moral expectations), it can be observed that this strong drive for corrective action entails that higher levels of guilt-proneness will translate into higher levels of individual task effort. Framed differently, workers who are comparatively 'more guilt-prone may work harder than their less guilt-prone colleagues' (Flynn and Schaumberg, 2012, p. 124). Indeed, in a series of studies, it was ascertained that more guilt-prone workers show higher degrees of attachment to the organization (compared with less guilt-prone workers), and that the link between guilt-proneness and affective commitment is mediated by greater task effort (Flynn and Schaumberg, 2012). For greater clarity on what this can imply in practice at work, please refer to Vignette 2.2.

In more extreme manifestations, guilt can reflect a sense of despair and inadequacy not found in shame. Even though guilt often represents self-reproach for some misdeed that may be accompanied by corrective action (an apology or greater effort), it differs in more intense manifestations from shame insofar as the guilty individual does not reproach him/herself 'only for [a] particular transgression but rather reproaches himself [herself] in general, as if [one's] existence is an offense' (Solomon, 1993, p. 259). So, when the notion of a 'guilt-prone worker' is invoked above, what I imply is what has come to be known as 'maladaptive guilt' – that is, 'guilt marked by inappropriate attributions of responsibility' (Kim et al., 2011, p. 74). I posit that these 'attributions' – and how they are instigated, produced and reproduced within organizations for political purposes ('political' in the sense of Rogers's view stated earlier) – mark a departure from appropriate to inappropriate ascriptions of responsibility. And it is in that move from appropriate to inappropriate ascriptions that the worker pays a personal price; that is, maladaptive guilt has stronger links with depressive symptoms compared with legitimate guilt (Kim et al., 2011), which involves accurate attributions of responsibility.[10] In addition, the experience of guilt also plays a role in the burnout process, such as when an

VIGNETTE 2.2: GUILT

Meet Jennifer, a 25-year-old deputy hotel manager. Jennifer is an only child, and has no child-rearing responsibilities. In the absence of siblings, the need for recognition and belongingness was naturally and mostly directed toward her parents. Her parents, in turn, had very high expectations of her in all aspects of her life, whether it concerned choices of school, how well she had to perform academically or with whom she was permitted to engage socially. Given these high expectations, Jennifer was bound to not always be able to meet these, leading her parents to express their disappointment. Thus, during her formative years, Jennifer became very receptive to the inculcation of guilt by her parents, whose frequent expression of disappointment made her feel inadequate to the core, as if she had to apologize for even having been born. Naturally enough, to avoid the experience of guilt and obtain a sign of approval from her parents, Jennifer developed the tendency to take appeasing and corrective action, promising her parents that she would 'try harder' next time during an exam, for instance.

Now Jennifer works in a hotel chain and has moved through the ranks to become the deputy manager. This is a remarkable achievement given that she only started to work for the chain three years ago. Jennifer knew very well that hard work and dedication got her into that position.

The manager is Alison, with whom Jennifer has worked ever since starting at the hotel as assistant receptionist. In Jennifer's eyes, Alison was incredibly charismatic in her appearance and approach to managing staff and the hotel. In addition, her eloquence and ability to quickly read social situations and act in order to position herself favourably were impressive. Small wonder Jennifer developed a deep sense of admiration for Alison and, like with her parents before, Alison's approval and recognition virtually 'meant the world to her'. However, Alison did not hesitate to express, even in the company of co-workers, her disappointment in staff (including Jennifer) when her expectations were not met. In fact, Alison was incredibly adept at eliciting extra effort – not through praise but by way of instilling guilt for having failed to meet her expectations. This effect was compounded by that fact that all staff knew that Alison's views on promotion or retention decisions would carry considerable weight in the decision-making process.

It so happened that the hotel was asked to generate savings by not replacing staff who had left the hotel recently (mostly due to low job satisfaction or ill-health). This, in turn, implied that existing staff needed to compensate for the shortfalls. Even though Jennifer could very well understand the implications of this, adding already one hour every day to her shift, Alison reprimanded Jennifer over the fact that she was 'disappointed' that Jennifer was not staying at work even longer to support her team. 'Would you not want to become even better at your job, and be the dedicated person and great asset to our team that we require now?', Alison asked Jennifer on more than one occasion.

Jennifer, knowing that each person's smaller contribution to the overall workload necessarily entailed that others had to work more, agreed to meet Alison's request. After all, she did not want to let anybody down at work. She even apologized to Alison for having had to be asked to put in even more effort.

After four months, the freeze on recruitment was still in place, and most members of staff in the hotel, including but especially Jennifer, felt demoralized and exhausted. But Jennifer also noticed that she increasingly lacked the motivation to maintain close contact with her friends and family. To her, that amounted to yet another 'chore' for which she simply did not have the energy. Despite this, Jennifer was still eager to please and receive recognition from Alison (as opposed to receiving messages of disappointment), though she struggled appreciably to convert that into concrete action at work due to deficiencies in her energy levels.

One day, during her commute to work on the local train, Jennifer stared emptily out of the window; the bushes, trees and back gardens that rushed past had an almost hypnotic effect upon her. Strangely and unusually for her, she was not screening her thoughts about work and of whether she would invest enough to avoid disappointing her co-workers more generally, and Alison in particularly. In that stage of mental quietness, it dawned upon her that maybe something was not quite right with *her*. She had done well professionally (given her position), but was far from happy or satisfied with her job. On the contrary, she was in the midst of burnout, and felt increasingly depressed.

Admitting this, Jennifer resolved to seek professional help from a psychotherapist. It was not a decision taken lightly, as she had always had trouble opening up and sharing her emotions and feelings with others. It would be erroneous, if not presumptuous, to suggest that the therapy yielded rapid results, but after months she understood what was wrong with her: it was her mistake to accept inappropriate attribution of responsibility for the situation at work. Instead, she realized that the organization did not resource the operation of the hotel from a staff perspective appropriately. She accepted responsibility to 'keep the show running' at work when, in fact, it was not hers. In sum, Jennifer understood that she needed to appraise the situation at work differently to more accurately attribute responsibility for the status quo. Thus, from an initial appraisal of 'I cannot let my co-workers and Alison down when they are already stretched' she moved to 'I suffer because of inappropriate resourcing by my employer.'

With the shackles of guilt inculcation by Alison removed, Jennifer handed in her notice at once to Alison – in person, and with small smile on her face.

excessive acceptance of one's responsibility assumes the role of a major stressor for the worker (Chang, 2009).

By raising awareness of the adverse effects of being inculcated with guilt by others (such as co-workers or supervisors expressing

disappointment about one's failure to fulfil performance expectations), the therapeutic effect of liberating workers from the effects
of inappropriate ascriptions of responsibility manifests itself. It is
noteworthy that the psychotherapeutic literature has long recognized
the debilitating effects of maladaptive guilt on mental health (Rogers,
1977).[11]

In summary, the emancipatory relevance of shame and guilt is due
to the abusive engineering of their social functions. In other words,
while I in no way wish to diminish their importance as moral emotions (Tangney et al., 2007), I want to advance the thesis that they
can also be engineered for the perfidious purpose of social control,
especially in the context of how we organize ourselves at work and
society toward particular goals and purposes (Holt and den Hond,
2013; Lindebaum et al., 2016).

2.3.1.2   Display rule around happiness

The consistent theme within Pathway I is that the social function
of a particular emotion is exploited in order to secure gains for
individuals or groups other than the worker expressing it him or
herself as such (e.g., management or co-workers). Although defining
'happiness' has proved intractable over the years in management or
psychological studies – for example, is it captured in job satisfaction
or psychological well-being? (see Wright et al., 2009) – Solomon
(1993) describes the accompanying affect as 'a buoyant breeze
that seems to lift us above the concerns of everyday', fuelled by
the appraisal that 'everything's *marvelous*' (pp. 275, 276; italics in
original). Recognizing these definitional issues, here I centre on the
function of happiness and its associated smile consistent with the
treatment of the other emotions discussed in this book. In this light,
the more general observation that conveying emotions to others
helps facilitate the coordination of social interactions applies to
happiness as well (Keltner and Haidt, 1999).

Key to the adaptive advantage obtained is the act of smiling,
as it can help form and maintain cooperative relationships with
others without running the risk of being exploited (Johnston et al.,
2010). Others add that happiness, and its associated smile, can help
establish social bonds and a sense of affiliation (Fridlund, 1994).
Not surprisingly then, the expression of happiness has been linked
to increased liking (Van Kleef, 2009). Therefore, the expression of
genuine happiness can be seen as an indicator that an individual

perceives the environment as favourable and benign, which may then signal to others that they are welcome, thereby initiating the social bonding mentioned before. In other words, if we are the target of happiness displays, we may infer that things are going well and that we may stay on course (Van Kleef, 2009). Therefore, the social functional perspective of happiness illustrates how potent this emotion is in influencing the strength and quality of social relationships.

Now let us contextualize this social functional account of happiness (i.e., increased liking and bonding) to show why it is relevant in the context of the contemporary workplace when display rules are at play. Consider this recent reflection:

> A Starbucks barista's job is more than just serving coffee. She also needs to be polite, even friendly, to the customers. If she does her job correctly, then maybe the customer will walk away feeling like the barista was actually happy to serve him – that it was not only her job, but a genuine pleasure. (Resnikoff, 2013)

This quote helps us understand why the social function of happiness appeals to organizations operating within settings that involve frequent staff–customer interaction. If the customer buys into the smile and the expression of happiness as being authentic, she or he may walk away with the feeling that the worker really liked him/her and that an emotional bond may emerge that will prompt the customer to return, for instance, to the food outlet for future consumption.

The economic value of a smile or friendly demeanour as part of one's job role was first identified in the much-acclaimed book *The Managed Heart* by Arlie Hochschild (1983), when she coined the term 'emotional labor', defined as the 'management of feeling to create a publicly observable facial and bodily display', adding that 'emotional labor is sold for a wage and therefore has exchange value' (p. 7). Grandey and Gabriel (2015) recently synthesized the vast emotional labour literature that has accumulated ever since the publication of Hochschild's book, suggesting that emotional labour comprises three elements: (i) emotion requirements, (ii) emotion regulation and (iii) emotion performance.

In this chapter, I focus on emotion requirements as part of one's job role or, more precisely, the role of display rules.[12] These have been defined as 'expressive expectations placed on employees as part of the occupational or organizational context' (Diefendorff et al., 2011, p.170). This typically involves an integrative goal to show positive and hide negative emotions (Grandey and Gabriel, 2015). Even though these expressive expectations can also pertain to anger – e.g., in the context of construction managers or bill collectors (see Lindebaum and Fielden, 2011; Sutton, 1991) – the majority of research focuses on 'happiness' in an established 'smile industry', or 'service with a smile' (see Grandey and Gabriel, 2015), ranging from fast-food outlets or airline crews to selling insurance (Fineman, 2001) and even university teaching (Ogbonna and Harris, 2004). Therefore, survival in service organizations is considerably dependent upon the successful presentation of emotional displays expected by clients and customers (Wasserman et al., 2000), as it putatively aids in completing the task successfully (e.g., the service transaction or sales pitch). To put this more bluntly, emotional displays become a matter of survival (instead of being a personal preference or choice) as one's wages and job security depend upon it. This firmly underlines the notion of an 'exchange value' with which Hochschild was already concerned.

It is, however, important to pause at this juncture and reflect on the very justification for display rules at work. From an economic perspective, Grandey and colleagues (2015) have recently provided evidence to suggest that displaying positive emotions to customers is not associated with customer purchase behaviour. In addition, stores that have been rated as 'friendlier' produce lower sales than less friendly stores, the reason being that in busier shops service workers tend to focus on being efficient rather than friendly.

The putative 'benefits' of emotional labour are furthermore undermined by the fact that expressive expectations that follow the application of display rules may pose difficulties for workers. Fineman (2003) provides here the inspiration to underline the excessive demand for not just 'being happy', but being exuberantly so. He cites an example observed on a television programme, featuring a conversation between a manager and a member of staff called 'Sal' in a fast-food outlet.

Manager: Morning Sal! How are you doing?
Sal: Fine.
Manager: Now look, when I say how you are feeling, I want you to say
            'outstanding!'
Sal: OK. [*She looks bewildered*]
Manager: So how are you feeling today?

Sal: Outstanding.
Manager: OK. Really get motivation. I'm telling all the crew today, when I ask them how they feel I want them to say 'outstanding'! Go like that with your arms [*He throws his arms outwards*].
Sal: OK.
Manager: So how are you feeling today?
Sal: Outstanding! [*She mimics him with obvious feigned enthusiasm*].

To better understand how this example of excessive exploitation of the social function of happiness in the context of work adversely impacts upon the workforce, it is expedient to explicate the two mechanisms through which this occurs: (i) emotional dissonance from the incongruence between felt emotions and need to display required ones; and (ii) depletion resulting from regulating emotions and their expressions over time and across episodes (Grandey et al., 2015). These mechanisms are the result of the presence of adverse workplace conditions, with the simultaneous injunction to comply with largely 'positive' display rules which come at a cost for service workers.

In terms of dissonance, it forces workers to display an emotion that may not correspond to the emotion they really feel when serving a customer (Pugh et al., 2011). However, workers can reduce the 'felt–displayed emotion' dissonance (induced by display rules) by altering the expressions of their emotion in order to be consistent with the displays expected. This has been termed 'surface acting', or putting on the emotional mask that is expected (Grandey and Gabriel, 2015; Hochschild, 1983). Surface acting maintains dissonance between the felt and expressed emotion. In a recent article, Grandey and colleagues (2015) summarized the current literature on emotional labour and the consequences for workers that can be routinely observed. They show that, in line with the dissonance perspective, display rules dictating 'friendly demeanours' are associated with somatic symptoms in the presence of incongruence between internally felt emotions and externally displayed ones.

Dissonance or surface acting also consistently predicts job dissatisfaction and burnout, and even spills over into worker's home lives in adverse ways (e.g., spousal/partner discontent). It is also particularly noteworthy that dissonance has effects upon the functionality of emotions, especially in relation to positive ones. For instance, previous studies show that the function of emotion is best secured if there is a match between behaviour and internal feelings. More exactly put, smiling while not being happy or maintaining a blank face when jubilant actually disrupts the functions of positive emotions (Lyubomirsky et al., 2005). The authors of the latter study explain that, for the functional outcomes of emotional behaviours, the relationship between behaviour and experience matters considerably.[13]

With regard to depletion, this tends to occur when emotional display demands on workers necessitate more self-control than they are able to accumulate, adversely impinging upon workers' self and their performance (Grandey et al., 2015). This approach is more consistent with another emotional labour strategy – namely, 'deep acting', in which individuals attempt to really create the emotions that must be expressed as part of their jobs (see Grandey and Gabriel, 2015).

The prevailing view on self-regulation is that 'the executive function of the self operates in a fashion similar to a muscle or strength with its available energy reserves depleted by self-regulatory exertions' (Wallace and Baumeister, 2002, p. 35, see also Christian et al., 2014). This stream of research demonstrates that the act of regulating one's emotional expressions also depletes resources (Vohs et al., 2005) and, therefore, has a range of negative effects on workers, such as impaired decision-making or physical exertion (Grandey et al., 2015). Fineman (2001, p. 225) also warns that relentless corporate injunctions 'to "really feel" fine, happy, good about the product, concerns for the customer' result in a greater need to engage in deep acting, which 'cannot be simply switched off at the end of the working day'. This incursion into workers' self-identity raises significant ethical and psychological questions which have been elaborated upon recently (Grandey et al., 2015).

Taken together, both emotional dissonance and regulatory depletion account for the adverse consequences emotional labour has upon workers, even though the costs appear more distinct in the case of surface acting. However, even in cases when workers align internally felt emotions and external expressions as prescribed by display rules, there are costs for the worker in the shape of physical symptoms, identity struggles and family conflicts (Grandey et al., 2015; Lindebaum, 2012).

Irrespective of workers being able to or feeling inclined to respond to the requirements of their jobs with surface or deep acting, the 'smile' represents that which employers will reward by paying wages to workers, typically in abysmally small amounts relative to the emotional strains experienced by workers.[14]

Control is hence a direct concomitant of being able to reduce the wages of workers, or even make them redundant, when management perceives that workers are not smiling enough – or not authentically enough (Cederström and Fleming, 2012). This is a non-trivial observation, for many workers will only have limited (if any) choice in selecting alternative careers given their skill levels.[15] In other words, they have little choice but to engage in surface or deep acting to comply with their job requirements due to pay and job security concerns (Grandey et al., 2015). But, as demonstrated earlier, doing so entails significant cost for workers.

Some critics might say that my depiction of emotional labour is very deterministic, as if workers are under such totalitarian surveillance that they can never lower their emotional vigilance in order to continuously comply with display rules. I am not denying that there may be some scope for lowering that emotional vigilance and be more discretionary in displaying genuine emotions. Of late, however, there are further nuances emerging in how service workers are compelled to comply with organizationally prescribed display rules, and these considerably reduce the scope for discretionary emotion displays. From a cynical point of view, one wonders whether it is no longer sufficient to control workers' behaviour by simply withholding or reducing their wages. No, the ultimate duress to make workers comply with display rules comes in the shape of peer pressure, which adds further complexities to the interpersonal dynamics as far as emotion is being played out at work. Consider these two accounts:

A 'mystery shopper' visits every Pret outlet once a week. If the employee who rings up the sale is appropriately ebullient, then everyone in the shop gets a bonus. If not, nobody does. This system turns peers into enthusiasm cops, further constricting any space for a reserved and private self. (Noah, 2013)

Last week I stood outside a fast-food chain interviewing a man who had tried to organise a union there. He told me how, despite the smiles of the people on the counters, the situation behind the scenes was about tears, stress and constant pressure. 'If the mystery shopper comes in and somebody is grumpy to them, the entire shift loses their bonus. Then everybody gets on to you: why were you grumpy?' It was an eloquent interview, followed soon after by a terrified phone call, begging me not to use it on camera. (Mason, 2015)

Given the low wages paid to service workers, it is no surprise at all that co-workers 'get on to' any worker they feel are bringing in less income only because of his or her 'grumpiness'. I cannot find any amusement in situations like these, for not only are workers faced with redundancies in an era of precarious employment, they also earn wages too low to sustain their families (let alone save money for the future). Add to this the effects of peer-pressure as a reminder of the urgency to smile and we are afforded a glimpse into an existence marked by despair, fear, stress and pressure to comply with the job requirements. But what is worth contemplating here is that these issues can manifest themselves because of emotions that co-workers express toward the 'unhappy' worker. That is, workers may feel intimidated or bullied by angry co-workers, or the unhappy worker may be forced to comply through prolonged humiliation and shaming on the part of co-workers who demand that one smiles his/her bit during working hours to secure a bonus for the entire shift. This particular point and many of the arguments presented above are captured in Vignette 2.3.

VIGNETTE 2.3: HAPPINESS

Meet Maria. Her family and friends loved her for her naturally cheerful and extrovert character. But she was also sensitive to the needs and concerns of others, offering support when need be. Three years ago, she moved from Spain to the UK at the age of 32. The reason for her move resided in the fact that her now husband, whom she met during a holiday in Spain (also three years ago), had a job with a reasonable income in the UK. They decided that, as a family, it would be best to settle in the UK. Even though she held a bachelor's degree in human resources (HR), and was in the top 5 per cent of her cohort, Maria struggled to find a job which corresponded to her specialization. With frustration mounting over the lack of successful job applications, she decided – as a 'purely tentative' measure – to apply for a position as a sales clerk at an outlet of a London-based coffee/food chain.

Relieved that she was invited for an interview, she set out to prepare for the event. She started by looking through the company's website, and it resonated naturally with her that sales clerks were expected to display specific behaviours – such as 'having a presence', being keen to 'create a sense of fun' or being 'genuinely happy'. She also noted that the website had a section entitled 'Things we don't want to see', including being 'moody or bad-tempered' or 'annoying people'. At that time, these references startled her somewhat, prompting her to ponder 'why do they perceive the need to emphasize the 'don'ts?' But she quickly dismissed this question as the reso- nance with the 'desirable' behaviours was too strong and she did not want to have the good news spoiled with probably unnecessary worries.

Being well prepared for the interview, she passed the 'challenge' with flying colours, as the assistant HR officer praised her. Maria, so she was told, 'had the perfect personality' for the job. Before formal employment could commence, however, she was informed there would be just one 'minor thing' to get past. The following week she was required to work in the outlet – on a trial day, so to speak. On successful evaluation by her co-workers, she would then be able to join the 'family' at that outlet. Again, not giving this 'formal requirement' much thought, her trial day turned out to be a 'promis- ing success', and she was able to sign her contract and start work in a busy high-street location in London.

During her first weeks of work, the 'local' socialization process was in full swing. Maria learnt, for instance, that to be perceived as part of the family it would be useful to be a bit more 'ebullient', and that she should not hesitate to provide (or receive) encouraging 'pats on the back' and to hug colleagues as part of the greeting/parting ceremony. In addition, she was informed that it would 'not be good' to have any lapses or discontinuity in her 'radiant' presence, as the company employed so-called 'mystery shoppers'. These shoppers would visit any of the company's stores at least once a week, and would then either grant a bonus to the entire shift if the worker in question serving them displayed proper 'company behaviours', or otherwise would withhold it. But not only that; the mystery shopper would write a report and would – without hesitation – 'name and shame' the relevant worker who failed to display the required 'happiness'.

In the weeks that followed, while still trying hard to fulfil both company and co-worker expectations, Maria noted the slow disappearance of her energy levels, and increasing alienation from her natural personality. She had always been a bit of a 'happy-go-lucky' character, but increasingly she felt that she was too exhausted to even think of this state of being. Once at home, she didn't feel like smiling any more. Over time, this impacted upon the quality of her relationship with her husband as well as with family and friends, adding further misery to her life. Small wonder her colleagues and line manager also pointed out – more regularly now – that she was 'under- performing' with regard to 'showing a happy presence' throughout her shift.

It so happened one day that Maria was particularly exhausted half-way through her shift, and it was in this 'off-guard' moment that she served one of the mystery shoppers. Two weeks later, all workers in Maria's shift received a report indicating that they were not receiving the bonus for that week as one employee (named as Maria) had failed to portray the requisite emotional dis- plays during one service exchange. Since the company would just pay the minimum wage, the bonus system marked for many workers (just as it did for Maria) an important opportunity to top up their salaries. All the more crucial, some of her co-workers were infuriated that, only because of Maria's 'failure' they had lost their bonus. Maria was made to understand, quite robustly, by several of her co-workers that they could not afford to lose the bonus again and that she had better make sure it did not happen again – 'or else', added a rather belligerent male colleague.

With the realization sinking in that she was continuously pressured by her company and co-workers at the same time to behave in ways that were increasingly to her disliking and disadvantage, Maria grew appreciably desperate to change her situation. Intuitively, she knew that this is was a self-defeating process; but improving or changing her current situation was far from straightforward. She had recently bought a flat with her husband, and the expectations regarding mortgage repayments were merciless.

Still, a few weeks further down the line Maria went to see her GP and was signed off immediately due to work-related stress, for four weeks in the first instance (renewed after this period for another four weeks). Maria needed time to recover and, more importantly, find the energy and motivation to orchestrate a new career path. With the support of her husband, she started to bounce back and developed a fresh sense of achievement. Her new job search identified an HR position in a company that operates both in the UK and Spain, so, given her background, she decided to apply for this 'perfect' job opportunity. She was delighted to be offered the post, and started the new job with a keen understanding to protect her 'authenticity'. Incidentally, she also resolved to greet any service staff in future with a sincere 'no need to smile for me' invitation.

In light of the preceding arguments, and to conclude the discussion of Pathway I to social control, it seems only plausible to invoke Mason's account again on the working realities of those workers in low-paid service jobs:

> Through the slights, insults, cold shoulder and dismissive looks, you have to keep on smiling, for the *modern workplace does not tolerate unhappy people* [italics added]. Now try keeping that smile going for eight hours. For complete realism, the next time you mess up – which we all do in our jobs – get your political adviser to stand in your personal space, and shout at you. Finally, go to an ATM and withdraw the trifling amount of £48.75. That's what [blogger] Maid in London earns for cleaning 17 hotel rooms in a day. Now imagine doing this forever.

2.3.2 Pathway II

2.3.2.1 Emotionologies and metaphors around anger

Within the context of this pathway, I propose that the evolved social functions of some emotions are increasingly overridden by the way we talk about 'the emotion'. In other words, I note an ill-guided divergence between the emotion (and the social function it can serve) and how we talk about it at work and in society.[16] Such is the contemporary character of this argument that we ran a symposium on this very topic recently with leading colleagues in the field (Lindebaum and Geddes, 2016a). To cite an example, the social function of anger is to redress injustice. Here, redressing injustice is both a function and consequence of experiencing and expressing anger (Lindebaum and Geddes, 2016b). Consequently, 'a world without anger would be, possibly, a compliant and quiescent world but not a just world' (Lindebaum and Gabriel, 2016, p. 903).

By contrast, a great deal of research labels anger as a negative emotion (Barclay et al. 2005; Bodenhausen et al., 1994) vis-à-vis the adverse if not destructive consequences in the workplace and beyond, such as aggression, violence, bullying, ineffective leadership or deviant behaviour (see Gibson and Callister, 2010; Lindebaum and Geddes, 2016b, for reviews). To exacerbate things further, some psychologists associate the expression of anger 'with an *urge to injure* some target' (Berkowitz and Harmon-Jones, 2004, p. 108; italics added). Others unashamedly characterize anger as 'a significant social problem worthy of clinical attention and systematic research' (Beck and Fernandez, 1998, p. 63).[17] It hardly raises any eyebrows when psychologists 'claim that they spend more time helping clients manage their anger than in dealing with any other emotion' (Kristjánsson, 2005, p. 679). Seen in this light, it is incredibly easy to label co-workers as having anger management problems. *They* have an issue in need of resolution.

But there is a need to pause at this juncture and reflect on whether this should be accepted a priori. Acknowledging the intellectual legacy of the late Bob Solomon, he argued that, while the talk about the emotion and the emotion *per se* are potentially valuable distinctions, scholars and practitioners alike have not always demonstrated an awareness of these differences, as indicated here (Motro et al., 2014; Waldman et al., 2011). As potential explanations of this lack of differentiation, I propose two relevant phenomena. First is the omnipotent 'hydraulic' metaphor – e.g., the angry person as a bottle when filled up and about to spill over (see Solomon, 2003). Anger as 'blowing one's top' is so pervasive that it still dominates our 'thinking' about 'feeling' this emotion. As Lakoff and Johnson (2006, p. 112) point out:

Metaphors may create realities for us, especially social realities. A metaphor may thus be a guide for future action. Such actions will, of course, fit the metaphor. This will, in turn, reinforce the power of the metaphor to make experience coherent. In this sense metaphors can be self-fulfilling prophecy.

For this reason, the metaphors around anger are no more than cultural artefacts that systematically mislead us in understanding our own and others' emotions according to Solomon (2003), though this metaphor is largely confined to anger. Second, there is what Stearns and Stearns (1985, p. 813) refer to as emotionologies, or 'the attitudes or standards that a society . . . maintains toward basic emotions and their appropriate expression; ways that institutions reflect and encourage these attitudes in human conduct'. It is noteworthy that scholars have previously commented that this phenomenon has rarely received any significant attention in management and organization studies (Wright and Nyberg, 2012; but see Lindebaum and Jordan, 2014, for an emerging interest). Key among the few scholars who have introduced emotionologies to the broader domain of management and organization studies is Stephen Fineman, who observed that emotionologies are generated and reproduced through a variety of discursive and organizational practices, with some enjoying greater permanence and potency compared to others. Yet, their pervasive influence in shaping everyday emotion and behaviour is tangible:

> We inherit emotionologies that soon appear natural and typically go unchallenged. They will inform how we should feel, and express our feelings, about ourselves ('happy,' 'positive,' 'fine') as well as how to feel about others – such as a love of winners, disgust for muggers, cynicism about politicians, and ambivalence towards teenagers. They shape and underpin the deference patterns of particular social encounters – what to feel or reveal at weddings, funerals, dinner parties, places of worship, or before a judge. (Fineman, 2008, p. 2)

Emotionologies develop both over time and space to define emotional standards for various categories of people (Stearns and Stearns, 1985). Thus, emotionologies reflect both a chronological and geographical dimension. In terms of the former, Stearns and Stearns note that emotionologies are subject to change over time due to a number of forces, including the media, advertising, popular culture, religious organizations, political parties, social movements and activist groups (Fineman, 2008; Wright and Nyberg, 2012).[18]

In terms of geographical influence, a recent empirical study across eight distinct cultural samples found that individuals endorsing values of self-transcendence (e.g., benevolence) wanted to feel more compassion and empathy, while individuals who endorsed values of self-enhancement (e.g., power) wanted to feel more pride and anger. In addition, individuals who appreciated openness to change (e.g., self-direction) wanted to feel more excitement and interest, while individuals who endorsed values of conservation (e.g., tradition) were keen to feel more calmness and less fear (Tamir et al., 2016). Thus, different cultures reflect different values in relation to the desirability of experiencing particular emotions more than others.

Taken together, thus, emotionologies both reveal much about the forces of social change and contribute to (or inhibit) these over time and space. In the context of work, attitudes toward emotion provide the expectations of emotional expressions in relation to specific issues, subjects or occupational groups (Fineman, 2010). They also, importantly, provide varying standards of 'appropriate' emotional expression for various occupational groups such as doctors, social workers or service workers (see Fineman, 2010; McMurray and Ward, 2014; van Maanen and Kunda, 1989), which is why this is so central in the context of this book. Emotionologies – or broader social conventions – shape, maintain and challenge standards of emotional expressions within organizations. Therefore, the important point to bear in mind is this: emotionologies represent a cultural variable (Stearns and Stearns, 1985) which, in turn, can have bearings upon the formation of individual attitudes and values (Tamir et al., 2016).

While both the hydraulic metaphor and emotionologies contribute to the distinction between the 'emotion' itself and the 'talk' about the emotion, Solomon warns about these distinctions becoming too sharp:

> Both are interpretations, and the same concepts often enter into the structure of each. Being angry may be one thing, questioning the legitimacy of one's anger, something else. But crucial concepts (e.g., of legitimacy, blame or responsibility) are just as much part of the anger as they are part of the questioning. (2003, p. 87)

He continues to argue that, in the absence of 'righteous' anger, it would be vain to discuss anger's legitimacy and/or value.

To recapitulate, anger's social function (and consequence) is to redress injustice; yet the talk about anger – especially in public discourses in the UK – oftentimes portrays it as a source of both individual and social disorder, including a catalogue of destructive consequences (Lindebaum and Gabriel, 2016; Lindebaum and Geddes, 2016b). This has significant ramifications for how we organize ourselves at work and in society toward particular purposes, for, by indiscriminately perpetuating these discourses, management researchers and practitioners deprive themselves of vital opportunities to allow the social function of anger as a force to redress injustice and unfairness to unfold.

This is no hypothetical or abstract statement. There are both theoretical and practical examples when, for instance, verbal abuse is equated with expressing anger: see, e.g., relevant policies in the National Health Service (NHS) designed to combat 'verbal abuse' (Lindebaum and Geddes, 2016b). Yet, when these attitudes and norms override the social function of anger, then acts of unfairness, injustice and disrespect toward others are more likely to remain unchallenged, thereby perpetuating the emotional 'pain' of victims. Thus, while organizations may seek to silence anger in order, for instance, to protect staff from verbal abuse, the implication of my argument is that, in so doing, they squander opportunities to repair flawed organizational practices and processes that harbour a variety of risks and dangers (see Vignette 2.4).

As I have argued before with other colleagues (Lindebaum and Gabriel, 2016), in approaching anger as a resource that can be both dangerous and potentially destructive, but also potentially very fruitful, I reiterate its two vital dimensions: (i) the informational and (ii) the energic. Both of these dimensions can be very useful in organizations. If anger is a brief spell of madness (as the Roman lyric poet Horace once proclaimed), there is not just method in the madness, but also a 'message in the madness' (Geddes and Callister, 2014). The information contained in anger is not unambiguous, and may need careful decoding and interpretation; both of these may call for extraordinary self-restraint, as exhibited by 'Thomas' in Vignette 2.4.[19]

Therefore, 'as a tool for organizational diagnosis . . . anger offers valuable clues about the stress points in a particular organization' (Lindebaum and Gabriel, 2016, p.913). For this reason, Geddes and Callister (2014, p.16) urge managers to 'move beyond an angry response and assess whether the employee's anger expression

VIGNETTE 2.4: ANGER

Meet Thomas. Now in his mid-40s, he is a self-employed carpenter, happily married to Lucy and has two young children. As a child, his parents were keen to instil in him and his siblings an appreciation of truth, justice and fairness, as well as respect for the dignity of others. While these attributes seem laudable, Thomas learned over time that they can also come at a cost, especially if they strain social relationships as a result of 'calling things by their name' or taking a stance for others when they cannot defend themselves properly.

On Good Friday some years ago, Lucy's mother's health quickly deteriorated, and she was rushed by ambulance to hospital. As a result of her prior medical history of bladder cancer, it became necessary to fit a catheter to relieve the pressure on her kidneys. After several hours, she experienced increasing agony as the catheter failed to work properly. It turned out later that the tube had got pushed inside too much so that liquids could not be drained. However, this insight would only emerge after a prolonged battle to have medical staff attend to the issue, as the further unfolding of the story underscores.

Thomas approached the nurses on duty to ask them to attend to the problem. Having externally examined the catheter, they stated that there did not seem anything wrong with it. However, Thomas picked up the point again that his mother-in-law was still in pain. The nurses' response was that a doctor would need to examine the situation as they could not find any fault with the fitting of the catheter from the outside. They added, much to the family's dismay, that the doctor was not working that weekend and would return only on Tuesday after the Easter break. With Lucy's mother's pain increasing, both Thomas and Lucy struggled to get to grips with this information. 'Why are the nurses not helping us here?', they wondered.

With her anger about the lack of help mounting in a situation of dire distress for her mother, Lucy asked Thomas to approach the nurses again with a view to something being done. 'I'm too agitated right now. Can you please go?', she asked. By now, Thomas felt the anger building up within him too, and he complied with Lucy's request to speak again to the nurses. It was a matter of utter frustration for the family that they 'couldn't get through' to the nurses with their beseeching appeals. Thomas put his now more 'affirmative' message across to the nurses at the main nurse desk on the ward. 'Look', he said, 'my mother-in-law is in utter agony, and you really want to tell me that there is nothing to be done until Tuesday? Are you going to leave her in pain all weekend? That's just ridiculous! There must be something that someone in this whole hospital should be able to do!' But he knew very well that he had to restrain himself, for just next to the desk was a big sign that Thomas had seen many times before in the public domain in this or similar form. In partially capitalized letters, it read:

> **STOP ABUSE OF HOSPITAL STAFF**
> We will not tolerate any verbal or physical abuse of our staff, and will take appropriate action against any offender, including prosecution in some cases.
>
> The notice was accompanied by photographs of security personnel, police officers and even judges and prison officers, thereby clearly conveying the possibility of punitive action if, in the eyes of the nurses, they were confronted with verbal or physical abuse. Next to the bigger sign was a smaller, complementary one encouraging staff to report all incidents of abuse to the security department and, if and where appropriate, the police. So, even though Thomas felt he a had a legitimate reason to be angry, he exerted considerable control to not give the nurses any opportunity to 'chuck him out of the hospital.'
>
> Still, the nurses kept referring to the doctor's return on Tuesday as a solution to the situation. Seeing no way to get through to the nurses with their urgent request, Thomas and Lucy phoned a friend who had undertaken prior research in the health care sector. She was able to identify a course of action that eventually led the nurses – once confronted by Thomas with it – to phone a matron from another ward who examined the functionality of the catheter. She quickly grasped the severity of the problem, and instructed the nurses to 'take the tube out, now!' It was then arranged to have the catheter properly fitted. On leaving the ward that day, Lucy turned to Thomas and remarked that she could not have controlled her anger in the way he managed to during his interactions with the nurses. He admitted to have struggled considerably himself, and both wondered what happens to vulnerable patients who do not have others to advocate on their behalf.

contains valuable information'. Thus, instead of an escalating spiral of anger, the information contained in anger expressions in relation to different breakdowns, frustrations and violations (e.g., a communication breakdown as highlighted in Vignette 2.4) can prompt a response.

Beyond containing important information about the stress points in an organization, anger provides a hugely valuable, though volatile, source of energy – a source of motivation that, if properly contained, channelled and brought to expression in constructive ways, can unleash imagination and the will to take corrective action in order to uphold moral principles.[20] Taken together, I contend that, by failing to distinguish between various elicitors of anger and their consequences, we become increasingly incapable of handling conflict at work in constructive ways.

2.4 'SEEING THROUGH' EMOTION AS SOCIAL CONTROL

The preceding sections have paved the way for a deeper engagement with the notion of emancipation from repressive social conditions in cases where emotion is that which constitutes this very repression. Therefore, having outlined both pathways to show how and why emotion can constitute a system of repressive constraints, we can now turn again to critical theory and its associated desire to emancipate workers or groups at work and beyond. The motivation for doing so resides in the fact that it provides an advanced sense-making device for both management scholars and practitioners to better put the two pathways to social control into context.

To begin with, although Freud articulated his ideas in the context of the psychoanalytical tradition, Connerton (1976) credits him (as if by accident) with suggesting a new procedure of critical reflection. More specifically, Connerton posits that Freud understood that the constraints which this reflection seeks to permeate are resistant because their 'weight is anchored within' the worker (p. 19). Considering the insightfulness of Freud's thinking justifies the inclusion of a more detailed description:

> Freud's 'subject' suffers under the compulsive pressure of restricted patterns of behavior and perception; he deludes himself about his own actions; he colludes, by internalization, with the constraints that have been imposed upon him. Only by grasping these illusions can the subject, as it were, free himself from himself: he liberates himself from the internalized conflicts which blinded him in his self-awareness and lamed him in his actions. [Consequently,] the experience of an emancipation by means of critical insight into relationships of power, the strength of which lies, at least in part, in the fact that these relationships have not been seen through. (Connerton, 1976, p. 19)

The above quote makes several key assumptions, and these gain greater visibility in the conscious mind once they are applied in concrete ways to the two pathways to social control detailed earlier. First, we are unable to step outside a habitual way of perceiving and behaving. Applied to the pathways, this implies that we are 'caught' in these pathways due to our failure to step outside these compulsive and restricted patterns and open up to or develop fresh ways to relate to the status quo; i.e., are there perceptual or behavioural alternatives available given the repression experienced? Worse still, we delude ourselves, collude and remain complicit with these emotional constraints placed upon us at work. It is, to use an analogy, as if a claimant were theoretically in a position to file a suit in court against the emotional repression that afflicts him or her at work, and yet she or he is entirely oblivious to the repression in the first place. In such a case, to use a 'literal' translation of a German proverb (*Wo kein Kläger, da kein Richter*), where there's no claimant, there's no judge. Taken together, we comply with, and render support to, those very conditions that keep us repressed. It is this travesty, then, that prevents us from 'seeing through' exactly how relationships of power at work prevent the emancipation of emotion in that context and beyond.

But before we can accept this argument, it is imperative to revisit prior works of critical theorists. For example, Geuss insists that seeing through power relation is only a first yet important step en route to emancipation:

> The emancipation at issue here must be 'real' emancipation. That is, it is not enough that the oppressed agents no longer voluntarily cooperate in their own frustration, there must be a change in the basic social institutions which does away with the experienced suffering and the restriction of human possibilities which motivated the agents to adopt the critical theory. (Geuss, 1981, p. 86)[21]

Along similar lines, others argue that 'social structures must be radically changed so that they actively support and facilitate ... expansion of purposiveness, creativity, and rationality' (Alvesson and Willmott, 1992, p. 437).

At the same time, it is also germane to remind us that an ontological faithfulness to social structure and relations may be laudable from the vantage point of ontological purity, but it actually serves to undermine that which it sets out to achieve (i.e., emancipation). In other words, the denial of self-determination and agency, along with the exclusive focus on changes in the social structures to foster emancipation, has *de facto* inhibited critical theory from unleashing its potential. For these reasons, I want to offer the thesis that the nearly exclusive focus on social structure has obscured the potential for what I refer to here as 'micro-emancipation'.[22] Indeed, Alvesson and Willmott (1992) have proposed this label before, noting that micro-emancipation focuses on 'concrete activities, forms, and techniques that offer themselves not only as means of control, but also as objects and facilitators of resistance and, thus, as vehicles for liberation' (p. 446). They furthermore note that 'loopholes' can be identified whenever/wherever power techniques are being exercised. Therefore, an attempt at micro-emancipation is an attempt to find such loopholes in managerial control. I construe this version of micro-emancipation as a little sense-making device for workers to be able to endure in jobs that are emotionally highly taxing without the desire being nurtured to actually change one's situation.

This view is also consistent with the idea that workers do not just leave their jobs; they can also stay to re-create and improve the conditions under which they suffer. And yet, in an era in which organizations exercise tight control over worker behaviour by having formal emotion display rules inscribed in job specifications (Lindebaum, 2012; Noah, 2013), attempts to re-create or improve these conditions can also backfire, as noted by Noah (2013) and Mason (2015).[23]

However, Alvesson and Willmott's (1992) version of micro-emancipation is different from the one I seek to advocate in this book. More specifically, my view is that, especially when that which exercises a repressive influence is emotional, promising and prominent gains toward micro-emancipation can be secured already by raising workers' understanding of what costs they are paying for remaining complicit in their own emotional exploitation. I propose here that the aim of micro-emancipation is *not* to seek loopholes in existing structures or arrangements of control and power. Instead, I conceive of micro-emancipation in terms of initiating and nurturing a critical mass of workers who are able and willing to start 'seeing things through'. Naturally enough, given any accomplishment of an emancipated critical mass, the transformation of others into necessary 'counter-normative peer groups' (Thoits, 2004) may then aid in the movement from individual emancipation to wider pockets within organizations (and beyond).[24] In any such case, it is likely to raise significant questions about current labour practices, where 'emotion' is the currency of the realm.

The questioning of such labour practices involving emotional labour has received explicit attention recently from Grandey and colleagues (2015), who maintain that 'emotional labor threatens decent work' (p. 770). In a quite critical article, these authors elaborate upon this by arguing that the requirement to engage in emotional labor (i) poses a threat to basic human needs and (ii) violates important justice principles.

In terms of the former, the requirement to engage in emotional labour threatens all three basic human needs – namely, the need for autonomy, for competence and for belonging (Gagné and Deci, 2005). The theory is that workers can only flourish in environments where these needs are met; that is, 'environments that provide some autonomy, opportunities for competence, and a chance to relate in meaningful ways with others' (Grandey et al., 2015, p. 773). Workplaces in which this is possible tend to foster well-being and performance, unlike more controlled environments. Strict impositions for emotional labour endanger all of these three fundamental needs according to Grandey and colleagues. To begin with, emotional labour endangers (through the imposition of display rules) workers' autonomy by imposing explicit controls over their self-expression of emotion. It also endangers competence by failing to appreciate the costs of regulatory depletion to task performance. And finally, emotional labour poses a risk to workers' need for belongingness by allowing disrespectful conduct by customers or clients with little means to sustain or restore dignity.

With regard to justice concerns, Grandey and colleagues state that formal impositions to engage in emotional labour constitute unjust practice. They argue that, traditionally, injustice has been conceived of in terms of: (i) inequitable distribution of resources (or distributive injustice); (ii) the allocation of resources by way of unfair policies (or procedural injustice); and (iii) as behaviour marked by a dearth of respect or dignity (or interactional injustice). Due to the low wages paid to service workers (ONS, 2015), employers appear to underappreciate the costs of emotional labour to workers, thereby unfairly distributing resources to those workers in high emotional labour occupations. Further, 'voice' and 'process control' are suppressed through the formalization of emotion display requirements placing explicit controls on workers' self-expression of emotions, which is a key feature of procedural justice. Lastly, through a strict imposition of display rules – and inherent sanctions for failing to comply – employers create the conditions in which workers are frequently exposed to disrespectful treatment by customers or clients, with hardly any means of sustaining or restoring the dignity and respect required for interactional justice.

The detailed treatment of emotional labour as threatening decent work is a suitable reminder as to why an exploration of critical theory is most germane in this book. As Alvesson and Willmott (1992) note, critical theory aims to facilitate the clarification of what the meaning of human needs is (such as the need for autonomy, competence and belongingness) and to expand individual autonomy in both personal and social life (see also Horkheimer, 1937/76). In the words of Fay (1987, p. 23), the ultimate purpose of critical theory is to stimulate 'members of a society to alter their lives by fostering in them the sort of self-knowledge and understanding of their social conditions which can serve as the basis for such an alteration'. I am reminded here of one of Solomon's sharp observations in relation to the experience of emotion. He argues that the 'technology of the experience' to discover the techniques and instruments to alter our consciousness 'from the outside' is the interest of neurologists or developmental psychologists – not his. Instead, he is interested in the 'politics of experience', changing oneself from within. He thus argues that 'to change someone else, whether for "better" or "worse", is, in a sense, to "destroy" him. But to change oneself is to *grow*' (Solomon, 1993, p. 125; italics in original).

Based upon these arguments, the inclusion of Grandey and colleague's work (2015) serves again to underline that I intentionally limit myself to identifying emotion as a repressive social tool. By way of referencing these prior studies showing the costs to workers as a result of that repression, I want to raise the workers' awareness that the current condition is psychologically and physiologically detrimental to them. If I were to remain faithful to the founders of critical theory, I would now be obliged to state 'what ought to be'. After all, critical theory is a normative theory, combining facts (i.e., *what is*) with values (*what ought to be*) (see Murray and Ozanne, 2006).[25] And yet, I shall refrain from doing so for one particular reason, which in itself is the subject of traditional debates within critical theory. That is, it is often neglected that *what is?* is already a value-laden question. As Horkheimer (1937/76) notes, what we perceive as 'facts' through our senses is pre-formed socially in at least two ways: (i) the historical character of the object perceived and (ii) the historical character of the perceiving organ (i.e., the reader, researcher, worker or indeed the writer).[26] He adds that both are not simply natural in kind, but are rather shaped by human activity, even though we perceive ourselves as receptive and passive in the act of perception. Therefore, it could almost be said – at least under some conditions – that the 'add-on' question *what ought to be?* at least partially duplicates that which is encapsulated in the *what is?* question.

Contemplating the potential practical consequences of this book, it is, of course, my hope that wider structural changes will follow; but prescribing what emancipated workers ought to do next runs counter to the potential of workers being autonomous, creative and spontaneous actors, which is a recurring theme in critical theory (Alvesson and Willmott, 1992; Fay, 1987).

Given the complexities of social life (and how it is infused with emotion), I am under no illusion that the micro-emancipation advocated here is straightforward or can be readily accomplished. I propose that a processual perspective involving at least two steps may be worth considering here. First, understanding that adjustments can be made to the way workers regulate emotion so as to lessen the impact of the emotional event upon them is key (see Chapter 3 for more details). But the really acute and pressing question then becomes for how long workers can accept and endure in the condition of emotional repression (as indicated above and in Grandey et al., 2015) once they can see through the role of emotion as means of repression? In consequence, the exploration of emancipation through the emotion lens is likely to also have enormous practical potential for workers and society.

2.5   SUMMARY

In this chapter, I have laid out how the social functions of emotion in themselves, or deviations from them, can be co-opted to serve as a means of social control. For this purpose, I have defined emotion consistent both with the key construct emotion regulation (as scrutinized in more detail in Chapter 3) and the notion of emancipation as featured in critical theory. In addition, I turned to the literature on the functions of emotion and how these manifest themselves across levels of analysis. The preceding steps enabled me then to introduce the reader to two pathways of social control. The motivation was to show how the social functions of emotion (or a divergence from them) can be enlisted to serve as a means of social control. Finally, I have joined these insights with the literature on critical theory to maintain that the social functions of emotion constitute a sophisticated system of repression the seeing through of which can potentially spark within repressed workers a desire to emancipate themselves from these conditions.

NOTES

1. Since William James (1884) many scholars have entertained the question 'what is an emotion?' Depending on disciplinary backgrounds and ontological positions, many attempts were made to define emotions. Engaging in this debate, while intellectually stimulating and often necessary depending upon the questions put, is outside the scope of this book. There are excellent prior works on this very topic already available as resources for interested readers (Elfenbein, 2007; Frijda, 1986; Keltner and Gross, 1999; Kleginna and Kleginna, 1981; Lutz and White, 1986). Instead, and consistent with recent studies (Lindebaum and Geddes, 2016b), I adopt here the literature on functional accounts of emotion, which entails its own conceptual assumptions.

2. Strategies, Solomon (1993) admits, can have a variety of effects. They can either succeed or fail, and can be more or less direct, well- or ill-conceived, as well as effective or, in some cases, self-defeating.

3. I note, however, that it is also consistent with the particular emotion regulation strategies as detailed in Chapter 3.

4. I define anger at this juncture for illustrative purposes. The remaining emotions of interest in this book will be defined later in this chapter through the lens of social functional accounts of emotion.

5. The differences in levels of analysis also require a more explicit recognition that these differences are also rooted in both psychological and sociological traditions. That is, psychology is concerned with the study of the mind of an individual or small group, while sociology is interested in larger social structures and associations among individuals and groups, and the kinds of social norms that can facilitate or impair human interaction within society. For the purpose of this book, it is of intrinsic importance to highlight that psychology also appreciates how individuals' emotions and feelings change in the course of a day, for instance (the so-called within-person variance). By contrast, sociology affords insights into how emotion norms dictate the (in)appropriateness of expressing emotions in the public domain, and the social consequences of it. Appreciating these two different levels of analysis is key to better grasping why regulating emotions differently in everyday life is so important in the pursuit of an emancipated life.

6. Even though Rogers wrote in the context of psychotherapy, the conceptual proximity with key tenets of critical theory is striking.

7. There will be some readers interjecting that shame, guilt and happiness can just as well be subsumed under the second pathway, whereas there can be instances where anger could be considered under the first pathway. I am not denying the possibility for this to be applicable in concrete social situations. For instance, I recognize that for very specific professions, such as bill collectors or construction project managers, anger can be an important emotion to display in the fulfilment of one's job expectations (Lindebaum and Fielden, 2011; Sutton, 1991). However, due to a lack of differentiation among different kinds of anger, and the associated negative public perceptions in relation to anger expressions in general (Lindebaum and Geddes, 2016b), I argue that it is theoretically more interesting to consider anger under the second pathway. Likewise, given the real-world examples enlisted to discuss shame, guilt and happiness, it is indeed plausible to consider these emotions under the first pathway in this book while keeping the option open that – under certain conditions – they could also be examined within the second pathway. Taken together, however, an examination of these possibilities or conditions is outside the scope of this book, and instead lends itself to future inquiries.

8. Note, however, that the theorizing presented here may also apply directly or indirectly to other emotions. Any such exploration is outside the scope of this book, and must be delegated to future research. As I pointed out at the beginning, this book seeks to open up conversation on this topic rather than conclusively settle or contain it.

9. Yet, caution must be exercised in 'lumping' these emotions together because there are distinct psychological processes at play for each discrete emotion discussed here (Gooty et al., 2009). Likewise, the social circumstances giving to each of these emotions vary. Therefore, it is necessary to offer separate treatment to all of them in the remainder of this chapter.

10. As one close colleague pointed out to me, this might resonate with some academic readers insofar as, on occasion or otherwise, 'others' will try to make one feel guilty for things one is not responsible for.

11. Chapter 3 will elaborate on this in much more detail in relation to emotion regulation strategies.

12. Emotion regulation is the key focus in Chapter 3. Emotional performance, in turn, occurs when employee expressions are congruent with job emotional requirements, or display rules (Grandey and Gabriel, 2015). Naturally enough, the very notion of emotion performance is something I would like to subvert in this book.

13. There is an irony here insofar as the social function of emotion is to help navigate an individual's social interactions and relationships. Crucially, this function depends upon the accuracy with which internal states are communicated to others. By implication, 'the more emotional behaviors match an individual's internal state, the better the social-communicative function of emotions should be served', while in cases 'when emotional behavior is dissociated from experience [as is the case with surface acting], social communication should be disrupted' (Mauss et al., 2011, p. 738). Thus, the imperative to engage in emotional labour, and surface acting in particular, constitutes a direct challenge to the social–communicative function of emotion.

14. For instance, a recent survey by the UK's Office for National Statistics (ONS, 2015) reported that the median weekly wage for the lowest-paid group – namely, caring, leisure and other service occupations – was a mere £341. The report in question employs repeatedly the term 'median gross weekly earnings' at its outset. However, when referring to the specific weekly salary stated here, it simply states 'median weekly earnings'. Though one would assume that the ONS applies terms in a consistent fashion (i.e., to connote gross rather than net income), it is not entirely clear whether this is actually the case. Either way, the salaries of staff working in the said domains are very low.

15. A combination of a 30 per cent rise in US labour hours in service occupations between 1980 and 2005, together with declining employment in all similarly low-educated occupation groups (e.g., production occupations, operative and assembler occupations, transportation and construction, to name only a few), would seem to support this claim (Autor and Dorn, 2013).

16. For the purpose of this book, I position this work consistent with research by Damasio (2000). He maintains that, while learning and culture can modify the expression of emotions and give them new meanings, emotions themselves are 'biologically determined processes, depending on innately set brain devices, laid down by a long evolutionary history' (p. 51). Making Damasio's balanced position explicit is highly germane since, as a topic, the emotion and talk about the emotion reside neither exclusively with social constructionist nor with more biologically informed perspectives on emotions (contrast, e.g., LeDoux and Phelps, 2000; Parrott and Harré, 1996).

17. To be sure, I fully agree that anger can be a destructive force. That is not the point; the point is a lack of justified differentiation among all types of anger elicitors and action tendencies. For instance, while personal anger may be elicited by an insult, with the subsequent action tendency for self-interested retaliation, moral anger is induced by perceptions that a violation of universal moral standards has occurred and that corrective action takes place to support others (for a review, see Lindebaum and Geddes, 2016b). Another problem is the conflation of anger with verbal abuse or simply rude behaviour (as defined by the eye of the beholder, not the person expressing it).

18. No matter what kind of organization is behind the proliferation of emotionologies (if only partially so), it often entails the use of visual cues planted in the public space (both real and virtual). Some time ago I started to take photographs of examples indicative of a particular emotionology whenever I come across them. Given my interest in anger and the public misconceptions often associated with its expression (e.g., 'verbal abuse' or 'anti-social behaviour'), I have documented these in GP practices, train stations, post offices, airports and even on the local bin lorry! And these photographs do not only indicate that one should not verbally abuse a member of staff, but they are also accompanied by an explicit threat that 'all abuses will be reported to the relevant authorities' (see also Lindebaum and Geddes, 2016b, for more background on the problems that these statements can create). Given these real-world examples, I fully concur with Fineman (2008) that we often inherit many emotionologies to the point where they indeed feel 'natural' and go 'unchallenged'.

19. I admit that this vignette focuses on hospital staff–patient/relative relationships rather than relationships among workers themselves or among workers and management, as is the case with the other vignettes. It has, nevertheless, relevance in highlighting that the conceptual parameters around Pathway II (i.e., a situation in which the talk about anger overrides its function) can be observed in organizations. Given the narrowness of the zone of expressive behaviour in relation to anger in some organizations (Fineman, 1993), I suspect that some organizations also have codes of conduct and associated sanctions (see Geddes and Callister, 2007) in place to virtually sterilize the organization against anger expressions.

20. That might be easier said than done, especially in a professional context – and I readily admit that. Imagine that your line manager expresses his/her support for your promotion one week, thus raising your hopes that the application might actually succeed, only for you to learn the following week that he/she now believes that 'you're not ready for this yet'. This is obviously a purely hypothetical case, but chances are you will get angry about the lack of honouring prior promises on the part of your line manager. You will probably want to wait a few days before you respond by email; but ask yourself how you would phrase the email. Would you write 'I was very unhappy about it' or would you write 'I was rather angry about it'? If Solomon (2003) is right in saying that our fear of anger is so visceral that its mere display prompts us to act as if there is a real threat of harm behind it (even though we know this to be incorrect), then chances are we take recourse to the first option. I am intrigued by the near impossibility in today's society and workplaces (especially in the UK) for individuals to say 'what you did there actually made me rather angry', even though one has a perfectly legitimate reason to experience and express anger. The emotionologies around anger these days are such that there will be probable damage to one's reputation among co-workers as a result of having uttered these words ('He/she has got an anger management issue').

21. The significance of the reference to 'changes in basic social institutions' by Geuss

(1981) and how that relates to the key arguments in this book will become more apparent in Chapter 4 (see Figure 4.1).

22.   Seen in this light, I strongly oppose the idea that any framework of individual psychology and therapy is impotent in the quest for emancipation, and that a solution to emancipatory goals can only be realized at the political level or through a struggle against society (Marcuse, 1968/2009). I recognize that Marcuse also stated that 'therapy could demonstrate this situation and prepare the mental ground for such a struggle' (p. 192); but, as indicated throughout this book with references to studies on self-efficacy, I harbour my doubts about this (ultimately) self-defeating stance. Somewhat curiously, I note that Marcuse is cited later as stating that 'a radical change in consciousness is the necessary first step toward radical social change' (Solomon, 1993, p. 8).

23.   Noah (2013) comments on the case of a worker in a fast-food outlet in London who was fired soon after he tried to form a union. The company in question claimed that he was fired due to making homophobic comments. Noah adds that the 'worker's true offense was being unhappy enough to want to start a union', and that, in a service context, workers are not supposed 'to be unhappy'. Apparently, 'the sin commenceth with the thought, not the deed'.

24.   It should be understood, therefore, that these ideas speak directly to studies on social movements and their interest in initiating, resisting or undoing social change (de Bakker et al., 2013; Goodwin and Jasper, 2006; Jasper, 1998).

25.   In terms of 'ought to be', some potentially interesting perspectives have been proposed recently, culminating in a call for a ban on formalized emotion requirements and a replacement of these requirements with humanist practices such as greater rewards for emotional efforts, organizational practices that support the emotional efforts and dignified treatment of workers (Grandey et al., 2015).

26.   As already underlined in the preface, this book is intended to be an exemplar of passionate scholarship, where my own life history (and its long-lasting interest in issues to do with fairness and dignity) is not kept at bay in fear of distorting 'science' but is rather integral to informing the arguments here in the spirit of normative theorizing and the values that these reflect (Suddaby, 2014).

REFERENCES

Alvesson, M., and Willmott, H. (1992). On the idea of emancipation in management and organization studies. *Academy of Management Review*, **17**(3), 432–464.

Asch, S. (1956). Studies of independence and conformity: I: a minority of one against a unanimous majority. *Psychological Monographs*, **70**(9), 1–70.

Ashkanasy, N. M. (2003). Emotions in organizations: a multi-level perspective. In F. Dansereau and F. J. Yammarino (eds), *Multi-Level Issues in Organizational Behaviour and Strategy* (Vol. 2, pp. 9–54). Oxford: Elsevier.

Autor, D. H., and Dorn, D. (2013). The growth of low-skill service jobs and the polarization of the US labor market. *American Economic Review*, **103**(5), 1553–1597.

Barclay, L. J., Skarlicki, D. P., and Pugh, S. D. (2005). Exploring the role of emotions in injustice perceptions and retaliation. *Journal of Applied Psychology*, **90**(4), 629–643.

Baumeister, R. F., Stillwell, A. M., and Heatherton, T. F. (1995). Personal narratives about guilt: role in action control and interpersonal relationships. *Basic and Applied Social Psychology*, **17**(1–2), 173–198.

Beck, R., and Fernandez, E. (1998). Cognitive-behavioral therapy in the treatment of anger: a meta-analysis. *Cognitive Therapy and Research*, **22**(1), 63–74.

Berkowitz, L., and Harmon-Jones, E. (2004). Toward an understanding of the determinants of anger. *Emotion*, **4**(2), 107–130.

Bodenhausen, G. V., Sheppard, L. A., and Kramer, G. P. (1994). Negative affect and social judgment: the differential impact of anger and sadness. *European Journal of Social Psychology*, **24**(1), 45–62.

Cederström, C., and Fleming, P. (2012). *Dead Man Working*. Alresford, UK: Zero Books.

Chang, M.-L. (2009). An appraisal perspective of teacher burnout: examining the emotional work of teachers. *Educational Psychology Review*, **21**(3), 193–218.

Christian, M. S., Eisenkraft, N., and Kapadia, C. (2014). Dynamic associations among somatic complaints, human energy, and discretionary behaviors. *Administrative Science Quarterly*, **60**(1), 66–102.

Connerton, P. (ed.) (1976). *Critical Sociology*. Harmondsworth, UK: Penguin.

Creed, W. E. D., Hudson, B. A., Okhuysen, G. A., and Smith-Crowe, K. (2014). Swimming in a sea of shame: incorporating emotion into explanations of institutional reproduction and change. *Academy of Management Review*, **39**(3), 275–301.

Damasio, A. R. (2000). *The Feeling of What Happens: Body and Emotion in the Making of Consciousness*. London: Vintage.

de Bakker, F. G. A., den Hond, F., King, B., and Weber, K. (2013). Social movements, civil society and corporations: taking stock and looking ahead. *Organization Studies*, **34**(5–6), 573–593.

de Hooge, I. E., Zeelenberg, M., and Breugelmans, S. M. (2010). A functionalist account of shame-induced behaviour. *Cognition and Emotion*, **25**(5), 939–946.

Dickerson, S. S., Gruenewald, T. L., and Kemeny, M. E. (2004). When the social self is threatened: shame, physiology, and health. *Journal of Personality*, **72**(6), 1191–1216.

Diefendorff, J. M., Erickson, R. J., Grandey, A. A., and Dahling, J. J. (2011). Emotional display rules as work unit norms: a multilevel analysis of emotional labour. *Journal of Occupational Health Psychology*, **16**(2), 170–186.

Elfenbein, H. A. (2007). Emotion in organizations: a review and theoretical integration. *Academy of Management Annals*, **1**(1), 315–386.

Fay, B. (1987). *Critical Social Science*. Cambridge: Polity Press.

Fineman, S. (2001). Emotions and organizational control. In R. Payne and C. L. Cooper (eds), *Emotions at Work: Theory, Research and Applications for Management* (pp. 219–240). Chichester: Wiley.

Fineman, S. (2003). *Understanding Emotion at Work*. London: Sage.

Fineman, S. (2010). Emotion in organizations: a critical turn. In B. Sieben and Å. Wettergren (eds), *Emotionalizing Organizations and Organizing Emotions* (pp. 23–41). Basingstoke: Palgrave Macmillan.

Fineman, S. (ed.) (1993). *Emotion in Organizations*. London: Sage.

Fineman, S. (ed.) (2008). *The Emotional Organization: Passions and Power*. Oxford: Blackwell.

Flynn, F. J., and Schaumberg, R. L. (2012). When feeling bad leads to feeling good: guilt-proneness and affective organizational commitment. *Journal of Applied Psychology*, **97**(1), 124–133.

Fridlund, A. J. (1994). *Human Facial Expression: An Evolutionary View*. San Diego: Academic Press.

Frijda, N. H. (1986). *The Emotions*. Paris: Cambridge University Press.

Frith, M. (2006). Stress and the city: alcoholism soars in banking. *The Independent*, 9 September.

Gagné, M., and Deci, E. L. (2005). Self-determination theory and work motivation. *Journal of Organizational Behavior*, **26**(4), 331–362.

Geddes, D., and Callister, R. R. (2007). Crossing the line(s): a dual threshold model of anger in organizations. *Academy of Management Review*, **32**(3), 721–746.

Geddes, D., and Callister, R. R. (2014). Message in the madness: finding value in anger expressions at work. Paper presented at the Academy of Management Meeting in Philadelphia, 1–5 August.

Geuss, R. (1981). *The Idea of a Critical Theory: Habermas and the Frankfurt School*. Cambridge: Cambridge University Press.

Gibson, D. E., and Callister, R. R. (2010). Anger in organizations: review and integration. *Journal of Management*, **36**(1), 66–93.

Goodwin, J., and Jasper, J. (2006). Emotions and social movements. In J. Stets and J. Turner (eds), *Handbook of the Sociology of Emotions* (pp. 611–635). New York: Springer.

Gooty, J., Gavin, M., and Ashkanasy, N. M. (2009). Emotions research in OB: the challenges that lie ahead. *Journal of Organizational Behavior*, **30**(6), 833–838.

Grandey, A. A., and Gabriel, A. S. (2015). Emotional labor at a crossroads: where do we go from here? *Annual Review of Organizational Psychology and Organizational Behavior*, **2**(1), 323–349.

Grandey, A. A., Rupp, D., and Brice, W. N. (2015). Emotional labor threatens decent work: a proposal to eradicate emotional display rules. *Journal of Organizational Behavior*, **36**(6), 770–785.

Gross, J. J. (1998). The emerging field of emotion regulation: an integrative review. *Review of General Psychology*, **2**(3), 271–299.

Haidt, J. (2008). Morality. *Perspectives on Psychological Science*, **3**(1), 65–72.

Henderson, M., Brooks, S. K., del Busso, L., Chalder, T., Harvey, S. B., Hotopf, M., Madan, I., and Hatch, S. (2012). Shame! Self-stigmatisation as an obstacle to sick doctors returning to work: a qualitative study. *BMJ Open*, **2**(5).

Hochschild, A. R. (1983). *The Managed Heart: Commercialization of Human Feeling*. Berkeley: University of California Press.

Holt, R., and den Hond, F. (2013). Sapere aude. *Organization Studies*, **34**(11), 1587–1600.

Horkheimer, M. (1937/76). Traditional and critical theory. In P. Connerton (ed.), *Critical Sociology* (pp. 206–224). Harmondsworth, UK: Penguin.

James, W. (1884). What is an emotion? *Mind*, **9**, 188–205.

Jasper, J. M. (1998). The emotions of protest: affective and reactive emotions in and around social movements. *Sociological Forum*, **13**(3), 397–424.

Johnston, L., Miles, L., and Macrae, C. N. (2010). Why are you smiling at me? Social functions of enjoyment and non-enjoyment smiles. *British Journal of Social Psychology*, **49**(1), 107–127.

Kaufman, G. (1989). *The Psychology of Shame: Theory and Treatment of Shame-Based Syndromes*. New York: Springer.

Keltner, D., and Gross, J. J. (1999). Functional accounts of emotions. *Cognition and Emotion*, **13**(5), 467–480.

Keltner, D., and Haidt, J. (1999). Social functions of emotions at four levels of analysis. *Cognition and Emotion*, **13**(5), 505–521.

Kiffin-Petersen, S., and Murphy, S. (2016). Ashamed of being ashamed: talk-inhibiting, soul-stifling feelings of shame. Paper presented at the 10th EMONET Conference in Rome, 3–4 July.

Kim, S., Thibodeau, R., and Jorgensen, R. S. (2011). Shame, guilt, and depressive symptoms: a meta-analytic review. *Psychological Bulletin*, **137**(1), 68–96.

Kleinginna, P. R., and Kleinginna, A. M. (1981). A categorized list of emotion definitions with suggestions for a consensual definition. *Motivation and Emotion*, **5**, 345–379.

Kristjánsson, K. (2005). Can we teach justified anger? *Journal of Philosophy of Education*, **39**(4), 671–689.

Lakoff, G., and Johnson, M. (2006). Metaphors we live by. In J. O'Brien (ed.), *The Production of Reality: Essays and Readings on Social Interaction* (4th edn, pp. 103–114). Thousand Oaks, CA: Pine Forge Press.

Lazarus, R. S. (1984). On the primacy of cognition. *American Psychologist*, **39**(2), 124–129.

LeDoux, J. E., and Phelps, E. A. (2000). Emotion networks in the brain. In M. Lewis and J. M. Haviland-Jones (eds), *Handbook of Emotion* (2nd edn, pp. 157–172). New York: Guilford Press.

Lench, H. C., Bench, S. W., Darbor, K. E., and Moore, M. (2015). A functionalist manifesto: goal-related emotions from an evolutionary perspective. *Emotion Review*, **7**(1), 90–98.

Lindebaum, D. (2009). Rhetoric or remedy? A critique on developing emotional intelligence. *Academy of Management Learning and Education*, **8**(2), 225–237.

Lindebaum, D. (2012). I rebel – therefore we exist: emotional standardization in organizations and the emotionally intelligent individual. *Journal of Management Inquiry*, **21**(3), 262–277.

Lindebaum, D., and Fielden, S. (2011). 'It's good to be angry': enacting anger in construction project management to achieve perceived leader effectiveness. *Human Relations*, **64**(3), 437–458.

Lindebaum, D., and Gabriel, Y. (2016). Anger and organization studies – from social disorder to moral order. *Organization Studies*, **37**(7), 903–918.

Lindebaum, D., and Geddes, D. (2016a). The emotion, and the talk about the emotion at work. Symposium presented at the 10th EMONET Conference in Rome, 4–5 July.

Lindebaum, D., and Geddes, D. (2016b). The place and role of (moral) anger in organizational behavior studies. *Journal of Organizational Behavior*, **37**(5), 738–757.

Lindebaum, D., Geddes, D., and Gabriel, Y. (2016). Moral emotions and ethics in organisations: introduction to the special issue. *Journal of Business Ethics*. doi: 10.1007/s10551-016-3201-z.

Lindebaum, D., and Jordan, J. P. (2014). When it can be good to feel bad and bad to feel good: exploring asymmetries in workplace emotional outcomes. *Human Relations*, **67**(9), 1037–1050.

Liu, S., Wang, M., Bamberger, P., Shi, J., and Bacharach, S. B. (2015). The dark side of socialization: a longitudinal investigation of newcomer alcohol use. *Academy of Management Journal*, **58**(2), 334–355.

Lutz, C., and White, G. M. (1986). The anthropology of emotions. *Annual Review of Anthropology*, **15**, 405–436.

Lyubomirsky, S., King, L., and Diener, E. (2005). The benefits of frequent positive affect: does happiness lead to success? *Psychological Bulletin*, **131**(6), 803–855.

Marcuse, H. (1968/2009). *Negations: Essays in Critical Theory*. London: MayFly Books.

Mason, P. (2015). Politicians love dressing up in hi-vis vests, but they ignore what's really happening to modern workers. *The Guardian*, 12 April.

Mauss, I. B., Shallcross, A. J., Troy, A. S., John, O. P., Ferrer, E., Wilhelm, F. H., and Gross, J. J. (2011). Don't hide your happiness! Positive emotion dissociation, social connectedness, and psychological functioning. *Journal of Personality and Social Psychology*, **100**(4), 738–748.

McMurray, R., and Ward, J. (2014). 'Why would you want to do that?': Defining emotional dirty work. *Human Relations*, **67**(9), 1123–1143.

Motro, D., Ordonez, L., and Pittarello, A. (2014). Investigating the effects of anger and guilt on unethical behavior: a self regulation approach. Paper presented at the Academy of Management meeting in Philadelphia, 1–5 August.

Murray, J. B., and Ozanne, J. L. (2006). Rethinking the critical imagination. In R. W. Belk (ed.), *Handbook of Qualitative Research Methods in Marketing* (pp. 46–58). Cheltenham, UK and Northampton, MA, USA: Edward Elgar Publishing.

Noah, T. (2013). Labor of love: the enforced happiness of Pret A Manger. *New Republic*. Retrieved from https://newrepublic.com/article/112204/pret-manger-when-corporations-enforce-happiness on 12 June 2016.

Ogbonna, E., and Harris, L. C. (2004). Work intensification and emotional labour among UK university lecturers: an exploratory study. *Organization Studies*, **25**(7), 1185–1203.

ONS (2015). Annual survey of hours and earnings: 2015 provisional results. Retrieved from www.ons.gov.uk/employmentandlabourmarket/peoplein

work/earningsandworkinghours/bulletins/annualsurveyofhoursandearnin
gs/2015provisionalresults on 21 July 2016.

Parrott, W. G., and Harré, R. (1996). Some complexities in the study of
emotion. In R. Harré and W. G. Parrott (eds), *The Emotions: Social,
Cultural and Biological Dimensions*. London: Sage.

Pugh, S. D., Groth, M., and Hennig-Thurau, T. (2011). Willing and able to
fake emotions: a closer examination of the link between emotional dissonance and employee well-being. *Journal of Applied Psychology*, **96**(2),
377–390.

Resnikoff, N. (2013). How companies force 'emotional labor' on low-wage
workers. *The Ed Show*. Retrieved from www.msnbc.com/the-ed-show/
how-companies-force-emotional-labor-low on 12 July 2016.

Rogers, C. R. (1977). *On Personal Power*. London: Constable.

Scheff, T. J. (1990). *Microsociology*. Chicago, IL: University of Chicago
Press.

Scheff, T. J. (2003). Shame in self and society. *Symbolic Interaction*, **26**(2),
239–262.

Schwarz, N., and Clore, G. L. (1983). Mood, misattribution, and judgments
of well-being: informative and directive functions of affective states.
Journal of Personality and Social Psychology, **45**, 513–523.

Solomon, R. (1993). *The Passions: Emotions and the Meaning of Life*.
Indianapolis: Hackett.

Solomon, R. (2003). *Not Passion's Slave: Emotions and Choice*. Oxford:
Oxford University Press.

Stearns, P. N., and Stearns, C. Z. (1985). Emotionology: clarifying the history
of emotions and emotional standards. *American Historical Review*, **90**,
813–816.

Suddaby, R. (2010). Editor's comments: construct clarity in theories of
management and organization. *Academy of Management Review*, **35**(3),
346–357.

Suddaby, R. (2014). Editor's comments: why theory? *Academy of Management
Review*, **39**(4), 407–411.

Sutton, R. I. (1991). Maintaining norms about expressed emotions: the case
of bill collectors. *Administrative Science Quarterly*, **36**(2), 245–268.

Takeuchi, H., and Nonaka, I. (1986). The new new product development
game. *Harvard Business Review*, January.

Tamir, M., Schwartz, S. H., Cieciuch, J., Riediger, M., Torres, C., Scollon,
C., Dzokoto, V., Zhou, X., and Vishkin, A. (2016). Desired emotions
across cultures: a value-based account. *Journal of Personality and Social
Psychology*, **111**(1), 67–82.

Tangney, J. P. (1990). Assessing individual differences in proneness to shame
and guilt: development of the self-conscious affect and attribution inventory. *Journal of Personality and Social Psychology*, **59**(1), 102–111.

Tangney, J. P., Stuewig, J., and Mashek, D. J. (2007). Moral emotions and
moral behavior. *Annual Review of Psychology*, **58**, 345–372.

Thoits, P. A. (1989). The sociology of emotions. *Annual Review of Sociology*,
15(1), 317–342.

Thoits, P. A. (2004). Emotion norms, emotion work, and social order. In A. S. R. Manstead, N. Frijda, and A. H. Fischer (eds), *Feelings and Emotions: The Amsterdam Symposium* (pp. 357–376). Cambridge: Cambridge University Press.

Van Kleef, G. A. (2009). How emotions regulate social life: the emotions as social information (EASI) model. *Current Directions in Psychological Science*, **18**(3), 184–188.

van Maanen, J., and Kunda, G. (1989). Real feelings: emotional expression and organizational culture. In L. L. Cummings and B. M. Staw (eds), *Research in Organizational Behavior* (Vol. 11, pp. 43–104). Greenwich, CT: JAI Press.

Vohs, K. D., Baumeister, R. F., and Ciarocco, N. J. (2005). Self-regulation and self-presentation: regulatory resource depletion impairs impression management and effortful self-presentation depletes regulatory resources. *Journal of Personality and Social Psychology*, **88**(4), 632–657.

Waldman, D. A., Balthazard, P. A., and Peterson, S. J. (2011). Leadership and neuroscience: can we revolutionize the way that inspirational leaders are identified and developed? *Academy of Management Perspectives*, **25**(1), 60–74.

Wallace, H. M., and Baumeister, R. F. (2002). The effects of success versus failure feedback on further self-control. *Self and Identity*, **1**(1), 35–41.

Wasserman, V., Rafaeli, A., and Kluger, A. N. (2000). Aesthetic symbols as emotional cues. In S. Fineman (ed.), *Emotion in Organizations* (pp. 140–166). London: Sage.

Williams, K. D., and Sommer, K. L. (1997). Social ostracism by coworkers: does rejection lead to loafing or compensation? *Personality and Social Psychology Bulletin*, **23**, 693–706.

Wright, C., and Nyberg, D. (2012). Working with passion: emotionology, corporate environmentalism and climate change. *Human Relations*, **65**(12), 1561–1587.

Wright, L. (1973). Functions. *Philosophical Review*, **82**, 139–168.

Wright, T. A., Cropanzano, R., Bonett, D. G., and Diamond, W. J. (2009). The role of employee psychological well-being in cardiovascular health: when the twain shall meet. *Journal of Organizational Behavior*, **30**(2), 193–208.

Young, P. T. (1936). *The Motivation of Behavior*. New York: Wiley.

Zajonc, R. B. (1980). Feeling and thinking: preferences need no inferences. *American Psychologist*, **35**(2), 151–175.

Zajonc, R. B. (1984). On the primacy of affect. *American Psychologist*, **39**(2), 117–123.

3. Emancipation from emotional repression through emotion regulation

Following a necessarily concise introduction of emotion regulation in Chapter 1, in this chapter I first delve deeper into Gross's widely used process model of emotion regulation, the theoretical assumptions it makes and the empirical findings related to it (see e.g., Graesser et al., 1980; Gross, 1998, 2002, 2013; Gross and John, 2003; Gross and Levenson, 1997; Gross and Thompson, 2007). In this section, I shall offer a review of specific emotion regulation strategies that are commonly discussed. Their discussion is germane, as the multiple strategies (and their associated tactics) available differentially apply to, and impact upon, the two pathways to social control introduced in Chapter 2.

I shall then explore the emotions discussed previously in the context of Pathway I (an excessive exploitation of the function of shame, guilt and happiness) in relation to specific emotion regulation tactics in order to show that they can serve as an immediate tool to assuage the costs of emotional repression at work. Note that this applies to workers who – for whatever immediate reason (e.g., sustaining the family or other financial obligations) – cannot leave their jobs straight away. In addition, this section outlines how one specific emotion regulation strategy can help remedy the costs associated with Pathway II (i.e., when the talk about anger overrides its function and forces workers to suppress it).

Thus, within these sections, I discuss how and why specific emotion regulation strategies theoretically apply differentially within and across Pathways I and II. The overall aim is to connect insights from the emotion regulation literature to the broader notion of emancipation through regulating emotions (differently) at work later in this chapter. To this end, I offer a conceptual flowchart as an expanded version of Figure 2.1. Finally, I synthesize the contents of this chapter to facilitate the transition to Chapter 4.

3.1   OVERVIEW OF THE EMOTION REGULATION LITERATURE

We humans are nothing if not adaptive. (Buhle et al., 2014, p. 2981)

This powerful claim underscores the fact that our ability to regulate emotion in response to the emotional 'pushes' and 'pulls' of our daily lives – such as remaining calm under duress or stress, rising resilient from ordeals or being able to negate harmful temptations – is of utmost significance (Lindebaum, 2015; Mill, 1861/2001). In the context of work, many employees do not face an abundance of positive experiences. Instead, they tend to experience more anger or frustration compared to being happy or enthusiastic. Further to this, the intensity of emotion experience – when we are, for instance, angry – is often more intense compared to other emotions (Lawrence et al., 2011). In the same vein, and more generally, we tend to regulate negative emotions (especially anger, sadness and anxiety) much more regularly compared to positive emotions in our daily lives (Gross et al., 2006).

If we recall how emotion regulation has been defined in Chapter 1 – i.e., the processes we can use to influence which emotions we have, when we have them and how we experience and express them – and if we apply the situations above (e.g., remaining calm when stressed) to that definition, it will become apparent that we cannot understand exactly how and why we could manage the situation in the way we did. In order to foster that understanding, it is first imperative to consider how emotion is generated. Theoretically speaking, emotion generation can be conceived of as a process unfolding over time. Emotion researchers argue that an emotion is induced when we perceive a stimulus within a context and attend to its features. Thereafter, we typically appraise the significance of the stimulus (does it matter to us?). Frijda (2013, p. 137) defines an appraisal as 'the process of detecting emotional meaning in information from an event'. Appraisals, in turn, activate an affective, physiological and behavioural response (see, e.g., Scherer et al., 2001). This framework helps explicate the sequential nature of the emotion generation process as applied in Gross's process model of emotion regulation (Gross, 1998; Gross and Thompson, 2007) as depicted in Figure 3.1 and further expanded upon in the remainder of this section.

Before I scrutinize these strategies in more detail, it is of intrinsic

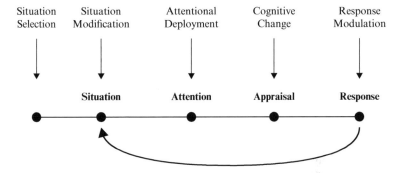

Figure 3.1   *A process model of emotion regulation highlighting five families of emotion regulation strategies*

relevance to understand that we do not just regulate our emotions in whimsical or random ways. Gross (2013) notes that emotion regulation necessitates the activation of a goal to either up- or down-regulate the magnitude or duration of the emotional response to meet a variety of goals. They can range from being specific (e.g., not showing one's line manager our embarrassment about his/her bad jokes) to being more general (e.g., behaving in a supportive or caring way toward co-workers). In addition, goals can be highly conscious and salient (e.g., when we want to avoid looking nervous at a meeting). They can also be rather less focal, for instance, in cases when they are influenced by the higher aim to do well at a job, which imposes adherence to feeling rules or display rules (Hochschild, 1979; Lindebaum et al., 2016).

Crucially, emotion regulatory goals are frequently context specific, such as when leaders regulate their emotions in order to meet followers' perceptions of situational appropriateness of their behaviours (Jordan and Lindebaum, 2015). Therefore, 'it is not the emotional response per se that is adaptive or maladaptive but the response in its immediate context' (Gross and Thompson, 2007, p. 15). It follows that emotion regulation can be harnessed to either improve or make things worse, depending upon the context or situation at hand. For instance, while cognitive strategies to dampen 'negative' emotion may assist a medical professional in dealing successfully with stressful episodes at work, such strategies may also lower or even neutralize negative emotion central to the eliciting of empathy, thus decreasing helping behaviours. In addition – and consistent with the focus in this book on functional accounts of emotion – emotion regulatory strategies may help facilitate the goals of the worker, while this may be perceived by co-workers or management as maladaptive.

Finally, and quite relevantly for the purpose of this book, goals can also vary by emotion. For instance, Americans have a long history of concern about anger management (Stearns and Stearns, 1986; Tavris, 1982), while other emotions such as surprise are less highly regulated. Taken together, 'the motivations for emotion regulation are themselves emotional. They often are as emotional as the regulated emotion itself'. In other words, 'emotions are regulated to the extent that one cares about the implication of having an unregulated emotion' (Frijda, 2013, p. 139).

In the context of emotion regulatory goals, Gross and colleagues (Gross, 2013; Gross and Thompson, 2007) distinguish between intrinsic regulation (i.e., when one's emotion is regulated by oneself) and extrinsic regulation (e.g., when one's emotion is regulated by others). In other words, we regulate emotion for our own benefit, or we regulate goals in order to respond appropriately to expectations of others. The distinction between intrinsic and extrinsic regulation of emotions is not mere conceptual luxury, but has profound implications for the pathways to social control, and the means proposed to render emancipation from these more likely. This is because the intrapersonal process of emotion regulation is initiated by social cues.[1] More specifically, all emotions of interest in this book (shame, guilt, happiness and anger) are regulated – in one way or another – by others (i.e., extrinsic regulation). As a relevant addition to this, Gross argues that 'it has long been suspected that the emotion regulation required by civilization [extrinsic regulation] may come at a steep price' (2002, p. 288).

Beyond the characteristics of Gross's process model of emotion regulation detailed above, he also explicitly states that emotion regulation is a dynamic and ongoing process rather than a one-shot deal. More specifically, the very act of regulating one's emotion in a particular way oftentimes alters the context or situation which gave rise to the emotion in the first place, and the feedback arrow in Figure 3.1 serves as an indication of this effect (Gross, 2013). The arrow underlines the dynamic and reciprocally determined characteristics of emotion regulation 'as it occurs in an ongoing stream of emotional stimulation and behavioural responding' (Gross and Thompson, 2007, p. 16). Similar feedback arrows may be drawn from the final emotional response to each of the other steps within the emotion-generative process, and it is noteworthy that each of these can, in turn, influence subsequent emotional responses. When applied to the context of work, this loop acknowledges the flexible characteristics of emotion and the possibility for emotion regulation to influence workers' dynamic experiences of their work. Put differently, the regulation of emotion experienced in any given situation may change the situation as such and/or the perceptions of the situation in some way. Felt emotions, in turn, and their associated response patterns are further modified. For instance, in terms of antecedents, which emotion we experience and how we express it are key inputs into new emotion cycles, such as when we feel embarrassed about a preceding angry outburst at work (Gross and Thompson, 2007).

Another central question in the literature on emotion regulation is whether it is a conscious or unconscious process. Even though prototypical situations of emotion regulation can be conscious (e.g., getting annoyed about co-workers not doing their jobs but refraining from expressing it to avoid making things worse), it is imaginable that emotion regulatory activities that are initially deliberate can later occur without conscious awareness (Gross and Thompson, 2007). While prior research has distinguished categorically between conscious and unconscious processes (Masters, 1991), Gross and colleagues prefer to think of emotion regulation as a continuum ranging from conscious, effortful and controlled regulation to unconscious, effortless and automatic regulation which can take effect at any stage (or multiple stages) during the emotion generative process (Gross, 2013; Gross and Thompson, 2007; but see also Grandey and Gabriel, 2015, for a discussion on this in the context of emotional labour).

If we want to understand now more precisely how and why we can remain calm under stress, or how workers can emancipate themselves from emotional repression (which is the ultimate aim of this book), we can usefully turn to specific strategies in place that can help regulate emotion. These strategies are encapsulated in the influential model of emotion regulation proposed by Gross and Thompson (2007), which serves as a valuable entry point for a more finely grained analysis of each of these later on (see Figure 3.1). The model reflects five points at which and how we can regulate emotion. This process model provides a framework for delineating different types of emotion regulation strategies:

- situation selection;
- situation modification;
- attentional deployment;
- cognitive change; and
- response modulation (Gross, 1998; Gross and Thompson, 2007).

Each of these points indicates a family of emotion regulation strategies and a movement through time within the emotion-generative cycle (Gross, 2013). The reference to 'families' implies that for several of the emotion regulation strategies depicted in Figure 3.1, several sub-tactics have been identified and empirically examined over the years (Denny and Ochsner, 2014; Gross, 1998; Gross and John, 2003; Lawrence et al., 2011; McRae et al., 2012).

The relevance of these strategies for this book varies, with some having more distinct ramifications while others only play a secondary role.[2] To organize these strategies more consistently with the extant literature, I follow Gross's conceptualization of emotion regulation in terms of antecedent-focused and response-focused strategies (Gross, 1998; Gross and Thompson, 2007). Both can be distinguished according to the stage of the emotion-generative process during which we attempt to influence this process. Of note: even though Gross's process model of emotion regulation has not been specifically designed for the work context, the outline of the various emotion regulation strategies that follows is infused with work-related examples.

3.1.1   Antecedent-Focused Emotion Regulation Strategies

Antecedent-focused strategies 'occur before appraisals give rise to full-blown emotional response tendencies' (Gross and Thompson, 2007, p. 10), including the cognitive, physiological and behavioural components implicated in this process. The focus is on manipulating the nature, intensity and/or duration of felt emotion. A relevant workplace example would be to consider an invitation to a much-anticipated interview as an opportunity to acquire more information about the company, rather than as a personal pass or fail test. In consequence, antecedent-focused strategies encapsulate (i) situation selection, (ii) situation modification, (iii) attentional deployment and (iv) cognitive change, for these aim to influence appraisals before full-blown emotional response tendencies are triggered. They can be considered at any particular points in the emotion-generative process for as long it does not go beyond cognitive change.

Despite their diversity, the common underlying theme is that these strategies aim to influence the character of the felt emotion that is ultimately experienced. In addition, an impressive body of research shows that antecedent-focused regulation is consistently linked with better cognitive functioning, closer social relationships and greater life satisfaction (see John and Gross, 2004, for a review on the evidence). This is entirely plausible; since antecedent-focused regulation occurs early, it can modify the entire emotional sequences before emotional responses tendencies have been fully activated. For this reason, it is key to preventing maladaptive response patterns. Below I unpack these strategies in greater detail.

3.1.1.1 Situation selection

Of all emotion regulation strategies, situation selection is the most forward looking. It involves an appraisal of the consequence of our actions, which aims to make it more (or sometimes less) likely that we end up in a situation we envisage will generate desirable (or undesirable) emotions.[3] Therefore, situation selection entails deciding whether or not to enter a potentially emotion-eliciting situation given the choice to do so. At work, it can involve deciding to either approach or avoid certain co-workers (e.g., a colleague one values or despises) or committing to tasks or projects that one finds more stimulating compared to other, more mundane ones (again, choice permitting). In extreme cases, it may prompt workers to leave their current repressive jobs in search of alternatives. In other words, situation selection is often characterized through the use of avoidance or confrontation strategies (Diefendorff et al., 2008).

No matter what strategy is pursued, what is required to this end is an understanding of the probable features of distant and future situations, and of the expectable reactions to these features (Gross and Thompson, 2007). However, it would be a mistake to assume that developing this understanding is a straightforward undertaking, due to significant gaps between the 'experiencing self' and the 'remembering self' (Kahneman, 2000). Looking forward in time, prior research shows that individuals often profoundly misjudge their responses to future emotional scenarios. For instance, they often overestimate the duration of their negative responses to various future outcomes (e.g., being denied promotion at work). This bias represents a challenge to individuals' ability to accurately envision future situations for the purpose of situation selection (Gross and Thompson, 2007).

3.1.1.2 Situation modification

Given job descriptions, assigned tasks as well as co-workers, it is frequently not feasible for workers to shun a potentially emotionally laden situation altogether or over the longer term (such as collaborating with an 'underperforming' co-worker on a joint project with joint responsibility). Therefore, a worker may attempt to alter the current situation in some way with the aim of directly or indirectly influencing its potential emotional impact (Gross and Thompson, 2007). For instance, one could seek the support of another co-worker to help adhere to the deadline for the project that is likely not to be met vis-à-vis the 'underperforming' co-worker. The worker may be keen to seek such help owing to the need to preserve or limit any drain on her or his resources.

   Unlike the modification of 'internal environments' (i.e., cognition – to be discussed later), situation modification focuses on changes in the external and physical sphere. On a final note, the vagueness of the term 'situation' can render it difficult to sharply differentiate between situation selection and situation modification. As Gross and Thompson (2007, p. 12) argue, 'efforts to modify a situation may effectively call a new situation into being'.

3.1.1.3 Attentional deployment

Attentional deployment marks a transition from situation-specific selection or modification toward a more internal modification of cognition. It typically refers to directing one's attention to a specific characteristic of the environment in order to modify that situation's emotional impact. It entails a manipulation of one's focus, which in turn can be achieved through the processes of distraction (e.g., turning attention away from an unpleasant situation at work), concentration (e.g., becoming absorbed in a different activity) or positive refocus (i.e., doing something enjoyable – see Diefendorff et al., 2008). For example, after a difficult encounter with a much-disliked line manager, a worker may focus on the next time he or she can pursue his/her favourite pastime. Alternatively, the employee may attempt to absorb cognitive resources by working on a more enjoyable task at work (choice permitting).

3.1.1.4 Cognitive change

Gross and Thompson (2007) note that, even after a given situation has been selected, modified or attended to, the emotional reaction is not at all a foregone conclusion. Rather, emotion requires that percepts be infused with meaning and that individuals evaluate their capacity to manage the situation. Cognitively inclined emotion researchers, as discussed before, have identified the cognitive steps needed to transform a percept into something that elicits emotion (see, e.g., Scherer et al., 2001). Cognitive change refers to 'changing how we appraise the situation we are in to alter its emotional significance, either by changing how we think about the situation or about our capacity to manage the demands it poses' (Gross and Thompson, 2007, p. 14). It encompasses a series of different sub-tactics, such as downward social comparison (i.e., when workers compare their situation with that of a less fortunate co-worker to alter their construal of that situation to decrease negative emotion), or changing the perspective from which one views the situation (Gross, 1998; Gross and Thompson, 2007). As an example of the latter, prior studies show that 911 emergency call-takers in the US focus their attention on giving advice and trying to view the situation from the callers' point of view (Tracy and Tracy, 1998). However, a particularly potent form of cognitive change manifests itself in the form of cognitive reappraisal, defined as 'changing a situation's meaning in a way that alters its emotional impact' (Gross and Thompson, 2007, p. 14). The personal meaning that workers attribute to the situation is vital, for it powerfully influences which experiential, behavioural and physiological response tendencies will be activated in that particular situation.

Beyond the laboratory work of Gross and colleagues (see e.g., Gross, 2002, 2013; Gross and John, 2003; Gross and Levenson, 1997), numerous studies have identified ways in which these tactics are used in a range of work settings. For instance, medical students modify how they appraise situations involving patients by regarding them as intellectual challenges and learning experiences (Smith and Kleinman, 1989); fire-fighters refocus on non-emotional aspects of their jobs and cognitively reframe the situation (Scott and Myers, 2005), while bill collectors cognitively reappraise the situation to facilitate emotional detachment (Sutton, 1991).

Multiple tactics exist to change how one thinks about a situation so as to modify its actual or potential emotional impact. Thus, reappraisal is simply an umbrella term encapsulating several discrete tactics. A comprehensive examination of these tactics has been provided in an experimental study by McRae and colleagues (2012).[4] Motivated by the notable variation in the effects reported in reappraisal studies, these scholars set out to examine within-strategy variation regarding cognitive reappraisal. More precisely, they considered the effects of emotion regulatory goals (i.e., increasing positive vs. decreasing negative emotion) and tactics (i.e., the kind of reappraisals actually used by individuals) on outcomes (i.e., changes in affective responses as assessed via self-report and physiological measures). Their study demonstrates that reappraisal can have different outcomes when individuals are pursuing different emotion regulatory goals and are employing different tactics. McRae et al. (2012, p. 253) conclude that 'reappraisals can be reliably categorized with [their] system', and encourage application to experimental and real-world contexts.

For the purpose of this investigation, I have singled out one such tactic that has the greatest theoretical relevance in the context of emotion regulation as a means toward greater worker emancipation from emotional repression at work – namely, distancing (McRae et al., 2012). This involves aiming for physical or psychological distance: 'this doesn't affect me', 'this doesn't relate to me' or 'I don't care'. Prior experimental research has demonstrated the utility of this tactic for reducing self-reported negative effect and less perceived stress in daily lives (Denny and Ochsner, 2014). In addition, qualitative studies suggest that psychological distancing can be a useful tool in managing possible tension between the need to perform well and be well at work (Lindebaum, 2015). For instance, one participant in that study (Nina) shared the view that 'work isn't everything to [her] at all' when asked whether success at work or happiness is more important to her, adding later that she has stopped 'taking work as serious' (p. 122) following the death of a very close friend (i.e., it changed her outlook on life to appreciate family and friends more).

Given these reappraisals, I propose that distancing is particularly relevant to the emotions of shame and guilt. Recall that these two emotions are so-called moral emotions related to moral transgression – either to prevent us from committing these transgressions in the case of anticipatory emotions or inducing reparative action to heal damaged relationships (e.g., offering a confession or apology).

Beyond these findings, prior research has repeatedly demonstrated that reappraisal correlates significantly with a host of desirable physiological, psychological and social outcomes. It is worth highlighting these in more detail at this juncture so that the full significance and potential of reappraisal manifests itself. For instance, there is growing evidence to suggest that emotional reactions can affect our physiological health, especially in relation to cardiovascular disease. As reviewed recently by Gross (2013), a key finding is that increased levels of certain emotions (e.g., anger or anxiety) predict worse cardiovascular disease, prompting researchers to speculate to what extent emotion regulation may be implicated in cardiovascular outcomes.

To test this hypothesis, studies have investigated the association between C-reactive protein (a marker of inflammation that predicts cardiovascular disease) and cognitive reappraisal, a generally more adaptive form of emotion regulation. Results suggest that reappraisal was related to lower levels of C-reactive protein (Appleton et al., 2013). Likewise, reappraisal has either no influence on or even decreases sympathetic nervous system responses, and entails lower activation in emotion-generative brain regions such as the amygdala and ventral striatum (Gross and Thompson, 2007). Psychologically, reappraisal has either no impact upon memory or correlates positively with it, and has been shown to improve exam performance (as summarized in Gross, 2013; John and Gross, 2004). Finally, individuals who regularly use reappraisal tend to experience fewer depressive symptoms, displayed greater life satisfaction, were more optimistic and enjoyed better self-esteem (John and Gross, 2004). Regarding social consequences of reappraisal, unlike those stemming from expressive suppression (detailed below), there does not seem to be a detectable negative consequence for social interactions in laboratory studies (Butler et al., 2003).

In addition to these crucial factors, reappraisal is placed centre stage in this book because it is used commonly in everyday life and lends itself to experimental manipulation (Denny and Ochsner, 2014; John and Gross, 2004; McRae et al., 2012). It is also a most relevant choice as the core elements of reappraisal are central to many forms of therapy (for more details, see Denny and Ochsner, 2014) and has shown substantial scope for change and improvement across life spans (Gross et al., 2006). At the same time, it is noteworthy that reappraisal is often no longer effective at high-intensity levels (Sheppes et al., 2011).

Given these characteristics, reappraisal is the natural theoretical choice to prepare the initial ground for emotional emancipation at work in the context of Pathway I, bearing in mind that emancipation seeks to foster the liberation of workers from (emotionally) repressive systems. These repressive systems (as represented by Pathway I) can entail considerable costs for the worker, as elaborated upon in Chapter 2 (see Grandey et al., 2015). While reappraisal is only necessarily a first step, I propose that it is from that step – over time and with repeated practice – that the disillusionment with the status quo eventually leads workers to explore different careers or organizations to work for (situation selection). If this momentum could be sustained, and more workers join the movement, I propose that this can then lead to the micro-emancipation explicated and defined in Chapter 2.

3.1.2   Response-Focused Emotion Strategies

By contrast, response-focused strategies 'occur after the responses are generated' (Gross and Thompson, 2007, p. 10). More specifically, response-focused regulation strategies are activated once an emotion has been felt and the associated cognitive, physiological and behavioural responses have been fully generated. Thus, if a full-blown emotional response is present (i.e., after response tendencies have been activated), we would refer to response modulation instead, for it occurs later in the emotion-generative process. Prior studies consistently show that response-focused regulation strategies such as expressive suppression – defined as inhibiting 'emotion-expressive behaviour once the individual is already in an emotional state' (John and Gross, 2004, p. 1302) – constitute a maladaptive form of emotion regulation and are related to the experience of more negative emotions, availability of less social support, inability to cope, impaired memory – factors which, when combined, increase the risk of depressive symptoms (see John and Gross, 2004, for a review on the evidence). In addition, expressive suppression impairs social functioning in the short and longer term (Lyubomirsky et al., 2005).

3.1.2.1 Response modulation

Response modulation refers to various ways of influencing emotion response tendencies once they have already been fully generated. More specifically, it pertains to attempts to influencing experiential, behavioural or physiological responses after response tendencies have already been initiated (Lawrence et al., 2011). Relevant strategies include, *inter alia*, expressive suppression; venting and interacting with others; and the use of drugs, alcohol, relaxation and exercise to cope with the physiological manifestation of the emotions experienced (Gross, 1998). In this book, I shall centre especially on expressive suppression. As outlined below, expressive suppression is of both theoretical and empirical relevance in studies in emotional labour and its associated display rules (as discussed in Chapter 2). Therefore, its relevance to the arguments developed here should be immediately apparent. Like before in the case of reappraisal, it is worth outlining that expressive suppression consistently correlates with a host of adverse physiological, psychological and social outcomes. Again, it is expedient to highlight these in more detail so as to render the link between expressive suppression (and its consequences across the aforementioned domains) and the theoretical characteristics of Pathway I more visible.[5]

In terms of physiology, prior studies confirm that expressive suppression is related to increased sympathetic nervous system responses, higher blood pressure and greater activation in emotion-generative brain regions such as the amygdala (Gross, 2013; Lawrence et al., 2011). In addition, while reappraisal is related to lower levels of C-reactive protein (in the context of cardiovascular disease, as indicated above), suppression is associated with higher levels of C-reactive protein (Appleton et al., 2013). Psychologically, emotions embrace a vital function in supporting memory (Bechara et al., 2000). When emotions are suppressed, individuals tend to end up remembering less information by virtue of the consumptive nature of self-regulatory activities (Baumeister et al., 2000). That is, because it is effortful for individuals to continually manage their emotional responses, these repeated efforts consume cognitive resources that could otherwise be used for optimal performance in everyday life (John and Gross, 2004). Further to this, individuals who habitually suppress emotions (e.g., when they engage in surface acting) tend to have lower levels of well-being, less life satisfaction, lower self-esteem and a less optimistic attitude about the future (John and Gross, 2004). With regard to social consequences, expressive suppression induces less liking from partners and is associated with higher blood pressure levels on the part of partners. In addition, the suppression of emotions has been consistently linked to inhibitions in forming relationships and rapport with others (Butler and Gross, 2009). Thus, a lack of close social relationships and support is a frequent concomitant of expressive suppression.

Taken together, antecedent-focused emotion regulation strategies represent a more effective and adaptive way of dealing with emotional reactions to emotionally challenging situations at work and beyond, while response-focused emotion regulation strategies often come at considerable psychological and social costs for workers. These are important points to bear in mind, as I discuss later the role of each strategy in relation to the pathways to social control introduced in Chapter 2.

Before I proceed to the next section, it is critical to clarify one key assumption reflected in Figure 3.2. Specifically, there is a certain asymmetry inherent in the flowchart in relation to happiness. While the effects of both shame and guilt can be mitigated by way of reappraising the situation via distancing, the same process does not hold for happiness. This is because thought processes around shame and guilt, while dependent upon social cues, are oftentimes internalized processes over which workers may or may not have control (Henderson et al., 2012; Kiffin-Petersen and Murphy, 2016).

By contrast, the expectation to smile, display a friendly demeanour and be radiant in one's appearance when serving customers are externally imposed constraints. Therefore, the effectiveness of workers attempting to distance themselves from an externally imposed and emotionally draining situation ('It doesn't affect me') remains questionable for at least two reasons. First, it still forces workers to match the emotional requirements of the job with truly felt emotions. Even though distancing efforts may be more effective compared with expressive suppression in limiting adverse psychological consequences for workers (e.g., in the context of surface acting), there would still be a degree of dissonance between the expressed and felt emotion. Second, turning to the case of Maria in Vignette 2.3, to distance herself psychologically from emotional demands at work is also likely to be improbable vis-à-vis the peer pressure she faced from angry colleagues to comply with the display rules at work (cf. also Mason, 2015).

In any case, it strikes me that there might be an interesting avenue emerging here for future research to examine in more detail the conceptual and empirical differences and consequences between reappraisal tactics such as distancing or 'reality challenge' – e.g., 'it's not real, it's fake' or 'this is just staged' (see McRae et al., 2012) – and appraisals associated with deep and surface acting.

Because the jury is still out there to ascertain these relationships, I advocate at this juncture that workers faced with excessive emotional demands at work contemplate genuine expressions of emotion within reasonable boundaries.[6] For this reason, in Figure 3.2 the arrow links the 'happiness' box to the 'genuine expression of emotion' box. Note that this link does not contaminate the purity of the logics behind Pathways I and II. The notions of excessive exploitation of the function of shame, guilt and happiness (Pathway I), or the 'talk about' anger overriding its function (Pathway II) for the sake of organizational performance or control, remain intact.

3.2 PATHWAYS TO SOCIAL CONTROL AND EMOTION REGULATION: FROM REPRESSION TO EMANCIPATION

3.2.1 Pathway I: Reappraisal in the Context of Shame and Guilt

Pathway I represents the postulate that the social functions of shame, guilt and happiness are excessively exploited for purposes for which they have not evolved (i.e., performance broadly conceived at work). However, it is theoretically germane at this juncture, as indicated above, to separate the discussion of happiness from the discussion of shame and guilt.

3.2.1.1 Shame and guilt

Examining shame first, it is useful to recall that it reflects negative self-evaluations based upon depreciation of co-workers or management for not meeting performance targets (Creed et al., 2014; Fineman, 2003). Previous research used a range of different appraisals to elicit shame. For instance, the Test of Self-Conscious Affect-3

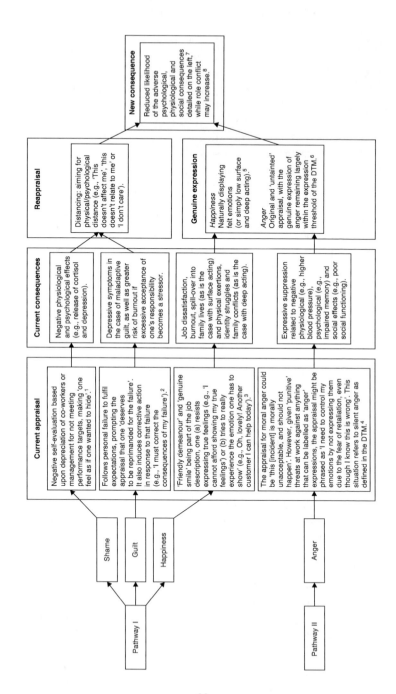

Pathway I

Current appraisal

Shame — Negative self-evaluation based upon depreciation of co-workers or management for not meeting performance targets, making 'one feel as if one wanted to hide'.[1]

Guilt — Follows personal failure to fulfil expectations, prompting the appraisal that one 'deserves to be reprimanded for the failure'. It also induces corrective action in response to that failure (e.g., 'I must correct the consequences of my failure').[2]

Happiness — 'Friendly demeanour' and 'genuine smile' being part of the job description, one (a) resists expressing true feelings (e.g., 'I cannot afford showing my true feelings') or (b) tries to really experience the emotion one has to show' (e.g., Oh, lovely! Another customer I can help today').[3]

Pathway II

Anger — The appraisal for moral anger could be 'this [incident] is morally unacceptable, and should not happen'. However, given 'punitive' threats at work against anything that can be labelled as 'anger' expressions, the appraisal might be phrased as 'I need to control my emotions by not expressing them due to the fear of retaliation, even though I know this is wrong'. This situation refers to silent anger as defined in the DTM.[4]

Current consequences

Negative physiological and psychological effects (e.g., release of cortisol and depression).

Depressive symptoms in the case of maladaptive guilt, as well as greater risk of burnout if excessive acceptance of one's responsibility becomes a stressor.

Job dissatisfaction, burnout, spill-over into family lives (as is the case with surface acting) and physical exertions, identity struggles and family conflicts (as is the case with deep acting).[5]

Expressive suppression related to negative physiological (e.g., higher blood pressure), psychological (e.g., impaired memory), and social effects (e.g., poor social functioning).

Reappraisal

Distancing: aiming for physical/psychological distance (e.g., 'This doesn't affect me', 'this doesn't relate to me' or 'I don't care').

Genuine expression

Happiness
Naturally displaying felt emotions (or simply low surface and deep acting).[5]

Anger
Original and 'untainted' appraisal, with the genuine expression of anger remaining largely within the expression threshold of the DTM.[6]

New consequence

Reduced likelihood of the adverse psychological, physiological and social consequences detailed on the left,[7] while role conflict may increase.[8]

Notes:

[1] and [2] Appraisals of shame and guilt adopted from Tangney et al. (2000).

[3] Appraisals adopted from Brotheridge and Lee (2003).

[4] Based on the work of Lindebaum and Geddes (2016) and Geddes and Callister (2007).

[5] Based on the work of Grandey and Gabriel (2015).

[6] DTM = Dual Threshold Model of Anger: in the presence of a very narrow threshold, it implies, by necessity, that the expression of anger will be perceived as deviant, potentially resulting in sanctions for workers.

[7] This indicates a short- to medium-term approach to secure the emancipation of workers. As I synthesize the contents of this book in the next chapter, I will expand this figure to include 'situation selection' as a potential precursor to generate the critical mass for micro-emancipation.

[8] Role conflict may then be the catalyst to leave the job, either because of organizational sanctions (e.g., being made redundant) or because the situation is intolerable for the worker.

Figure 3.2   Pathways to social control and emotion regulation: current and new consequences

(TOSCA-3) by Tangney and colleagues (2000) uses the appraisal 'you would feel as if you wanted to hide' following making a mistake (or simply underperforming) at work, which adversely impacts upon other co-workers. Accepting this appraisal and its legitimacy can lead to a host of adverse physiological and psychological consequences, as alluded to earlier.

True to the spirit of this book, it is of fundamental importance that the situation is reappraised so as to change a situation's meaning in a way that alters its emotional impact. As indicated before and in Figure 3.2, I propose the use of distancing as a reappraisal tactic for the emotion of shame, which aims to establish psychological distance between the worker and the shame-eliciting event. It does so – on a more abstract level – by using appraisals such as 'this doesn't affect me', 'this doesn't relate to me' or 'I don't care'. However, once the above appraisals are contextualized – for instance, with the notorious cabbage example – the need for a modification arises such that 'this doesn't affect me as it is not legitimate and decent practice' or 'I don't care because this episode tells me more about them rather than me'.

Turning to guilt, it is worth recalling that it has been described as an unpleasant emotion that follows personal failure to fulfil expectations (Flynn and Schaumberg, 2012). In terms of functional action orientation (Tangney, 1990), guilt-prone workers tend to feel a sense of urgency in taking corrective action in response to personal failure. These aspects are reflected in available psychometric instruments which offer several appraisals to examine guilt (slightly amended here), one pertinent example being that one 'deserve[s] to be reprimanded for the failure' and that one 'must correct the consequences of one's failure' (see Tangney et al., 2000).

While vital in correcting moral wrongdoings, consistent with the parameters of Pathway I, the social function of guilt can also be subverted for organizational benefits, especially if it takes the shape of maladaptive guilt (i.e., guilt marked by inappropriate attributions of responsibility). In other words, one incorrectly assumes the deservingness or legitimacy of the reprimand when, in fact, one does not need to.[7] As noted before, guilt-prone workers are highly motivated to make amends and will exert considerable energy toward this end. Considering guilt in terms of failure to fulfil performance expectations at work (as opposed to failure to meet moral expectations), it becomes clear that this strong drive for corrective action entails that higher levels of guilt-proneness will translate into higher levels of individual task effort (Flynn and Schaumberg, 2012). However, it is in the move from appropriate to inappropriate attributions of guilt that the worker pays a personal price, because maladaptive guilt has stronger links with depressive symptoms compared with legitimate guilt, which involves accurate attributions of responsibility (see Kim et al., 2011). In addition, the experience of guilt also plays a role in the burnout process, such as when an excessive acceptance of one's responsibility assumes the role of a major stressor for the worker (Chang, 2009).

Similar to the outline of shame above, the use of distancing as a reappraisal tactic applies to the emotion of guilt as well. Again assuming a more contextually informed appraisal (based upon Vignette 2.2 around Jennifer), psychological distancing can be achieved by using appraisals such as 'I don't care any more, as I suffer thanks to my employer's inappropriate resourcing'.

Combining the perspectives on shame and guilt detailed in the preceding sections, these modified appraisals (based upon psychological distancing) entail two central insights:

- They signal that workers can start to 'see through' the power relations at work that have a repressive effect upon them.
- Workers can start building a psychological buffer to protect themselves – in the short run – against the psychological and physiological costs that the acceptance of the legitimacy of shame- or guilt-eliciting events has upon them.

I do wonder, however, for how long workers (again, given a choice) would stay in such emotionally repressive situations once they can see through the repression. To what extent can this then lead to situation selection (i.e., an antecedent-focused emotion regulation strategy) when, for instance, workers leave their jobs? If this movement reaches critical mass (e.g., when staff turnover reaches unsustainable levels for organizations), can this then initiate the micro-emancipation that I have proposed before – that is, micro-emancipation in terms of initiating and nurturing a critical mass of workers who are able and willing to start 'seeing things through'? I believe that these questions represent an intriguing conundrum to explore in future research.

3.2.1.2 Genuine expression of happiness

Unlike shame and guilt, where the appraisal is more internal, it is the external expectation to smile and be radiant at work that requires an exploration of the mechanisms through which emancipation from these repressive conditions can be achieved. With job descriptions stipulating a narrow range of expected behaviours around emotional requirements, as dictated by display rules (see, e.g., Lindebaum, 2012; Noah, 2013), workers are said to have to engage in surface acting (resisting expressing one's true feelings) or deep acting (when one really experiences the emotion one has to show). Partly turning to Brotheridge and Lee (2003) for inspiration on relevant appraisals, 'I cannot afford showing my true feelings' is indicative of surface acting, while 'Oh, lovely! Another customer I can help today!' is an appraisal consistent with deep acting (see, e.g., Grandey, 2000).

Recall that job dissatisfaction, burnout and spill-over into family lives have been associated with surface acting, while physical exertion, identity struggles and family conflicts are consequences linked with deep acting. To insulate workers from these adverse consequences, I advocate the genuine expression of felt emotion, which has been said recently to simply reflect low surface or deep acting (Grandey and Gabriel, 2015). I also submit that, from an ethical and emancipatory perspective, organizations should not be able to impose formalized emotion display rules at work upon workers. Indeed, such was the emphatic message in a recent article by Grandey and colleagues (2015) when they argued that 'emotional labor threatens decent work' (p. 770) because (i) the benefits of imposing emotional labour do not outweigh the costs; (ii) emotional labour violates fair salary practices; and (iii) emotional labour violates the dignity of workers. For these reasons, they advocate a ban on formalized emotion display rules at work, and replace instead emotion display rules with humanistic practices. The latter includes rewarding emotional labour proportionately to the emotional effort; implementing organizational practices that are perceived as supporting workers (as opposed to yet more 'control'); and interpersonal treatment at work that signals dignity for and to all.[8]

It strikes me that these proposals may put the conditions into place for the kind of micro-emancipation as articulated by Alvesson and Willmott (1992) – namely, the seeking of loopholes to evade manage- rial control. Whether or not workers actually express their genuine emotions despite emotional demands to the contrary is contingent upon changes in appraisals that follow from having 'seen through' the repression (see Connerton, 1976, and Chapter 1, this volume). If the appraisal (e.g., 'That's it – enough is enough!') is coupled with high self-efficacy, need for growth and autonomy, it is more likely that workers will eventually leave their rotten jobs. Whether they do so immediately or only after having orchestrated a professional alternative would depend upon the degree of choice they have at a particular moment in time (given the need to support their family or other financial obligations). Consistent with the emotion regulation strategies outlined before, any situation where a worker would actually leave the job would constitute an act of situation selection.

3.2.2   Pathway II: Genuine Expression of Anger

As a brief reminder, the key characteristic of Pathway II is that there is divergence between 'anger' (and the function it can serve) and the 'talk about it' as signified by emotionologies and metaphors about anger. To put this more succinctly, the latter overrides the former. While previous research has highlighted and empirically examined various kinds of anger and associated elicitors (Batson et al., 2007; Geddes and Callister, 2007; Gibson and Callister, 2010; Montada and Schneider, 1989; O'Mara et al., 2011), what Deanna Geddes and I have criticized recently is a lack of sufficient theoretical and practical differentiation among various kinds of anger and related constructs. This unfortunate situation basically equates anger and its expression – even when appropriate under the circumstances – with hostility, aggression or verbal abuse, thereby conflating the emotion of anger with both harmful intent and damaging consequences (Lindebaum and Geddes, 2016).

However, I have explicitly invoked the functional approach to the study of anger, according to which the social function of anger is to redress injustice. As we have argued, this more moral connotation implies that (i) universal moral standards are violated, (ii) we feel concern for others and (iii) we take corrective action (Lindebaum and Geddes, 2016). It is in this strict moral sense that I advocate here that workers should be encouraged and less hesitant to express this kind of anger. Inversely, I want to be very clear here that I do not advocate the idea that workers should simply vent any anger irrespective of the consequences for them, their co-workers or the organization they work for. After all, Aristotle already recognized that:

> Anyone can get angry–that is easy . . . but to do this to the right person, to the right extent, at the right time, with the right motive, and in the right way, that is not for everyone, nor is it easy. (cited in Geddes and Callister, 2007, p. 721)

I have detailed above already that emotion suppression is related to a plethora of negative physiological and psychological consequences. And yet, I shall elaborate a little further upon these consequences, especially why this plays a significant role if the appraisal of a moral standard violation is implicated about which the worker cares deeply. This point is inspired by the work of Pennebaker (1982) and his important study on the benefits of expressing emotion. He maintains that the most important predictor of whether silencing emotional expression is healthy or unhealthy to individuals (or the worker here) is their conflict over its expression. For the individual, Pennebaker contends that detrimental results are more likely when they have a need to talk about an event but consciously and actively hold back the expression and mask their feelings. The inverse conclusion is such that results may be even more detrimental when workers want to express their emotion but feel compelled to silence their anger due to fear of negative organizational or personal ramifications, unlike silence stemming from their own preference or strategic choices (Geddes and Lindebaum, forthcoming).

As a theoretical framework to explicate the transition from emotional repression to emancipation in the case of anger, I draw upon the highly influential Dual Threshold Model of Anger (DTM) proposed by Geddes and Callister (2007) and indicated in Figure 3.3.

In recent years, this model has gained prominence in studies on workplace anger (Barling et al., 2008; Geddes and Callister, 2014; Gibson and Callister, 2010; Jordan and Lindebaum, 2015; Van Kleef et al., 2012). Consistent with a functional perspective on anger advocated here, this model helps to examine the (dys)functionality of anger in the workplace, for it provides the means of distilling three forms of anger: (i) suppressed, (ii) expressed and (iii) deviant. These forms of anger represent a function of two thresholds at play: (i) the expression threshold and (ii) the impropriety threshold. To elaborate, suppressed anger reflects anger that does not cross the expression threshold. It includes two levels, the first being silent anger (cf. 'anger-in' in Domagalski and Steelman, 2005). It is an intrapersonal phenomenon, reflecting that workers recognize their anger but inhibit the outward expression thereof. For this reason, it is distinct from muted anger (the second level), which is interpersonal in kind because the anger is expressed but 'misdirected'. In other words, the anger is expressed to 'non-relevant' others – as opposed to co-workers or managers responsible for the anger experience. By implication, workers

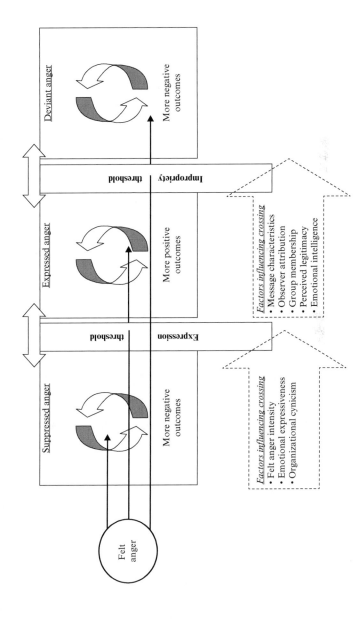

Source: Geddes and Callister (2007, p. 723), with permission of the authors.

Figure 3.3 The Dual Threshold Model of Anger (DTM) in organizations

express their anger to others with whom they have a relationship but are nonetheless powerless to improve the situation.

Moving to the right in the DTM, expressed anger is in direct opposition to suppressed anger, and occurs when workers convey their felt anger to organizational members who are responsible for resolving, or are able to take appropriate action to help resolve, a problematic situation. Thus, anger is expressed to relevant others. Where this occurs, it is said that the expression threshold is crossed. However, to remain within the space between the expression and impropriety thresholds, the expression of anger must be expressed in a manner which is considered legitimate and appropriate by organizational observers (Geddes and Callister, 2007). In other words, the expression remains within organizational boundaries of propriety. In this regard, Geddes and Callister (2007) very usefully invoke the work of Fineman (1993, p. 218) and his notion of the 'zone of expressive tolerance'. This space will often vary and can be expanded or contracted in response to organizational members modifying, relaxing or reinforcing norms to do with anger.

Continuing the DTM to the right, crossing the impropriety threshold implies that the expression of anger has been perceived as violating or deviating from social and organizational norms. In such cases, it is possible that deviant anger can generate 'spirals of incivility' or increase the likelihood of aggression (Geddes and Callister, 2007).

Overall, the propensity for anger to be deviant or functional, and thus detrimental/beneficial to workers and organizations, is dependent upon the congruence of the expression of anger with display rules and norms (Gibson and Callister, 2010). These being informed, in turn, by organizational climate, culture and policies, it is plausible to suggest that emotionologies and metaphors about anger potentially do feed into them.[9]

If I apply the insights from the DTM to the theorizing developed here, a conundrum emerges. If one assumes that the zone of expressive tolerance (the space between the expression and impropriety threshold) is wide, it should be theoretically more likely that workers can express morally motivated anger without observers deeming it inappropriate, as violating organizational norms. But the key premise of the DTM is that deviant anger is an observer-driven phenomenon (Geddes and Callister, 2007). So if current emotionologies and metaphors around anger influence organizational norms in such a way that the zone of expressive tolerance contracts sharply (for elaborations on the causes and consequences of this, see Lindebaum and Gabriel, 2016; Lindebaum and Geddes, 2016), then workers face a difficult choice: can they balance the desire to speak out about moral trans- gressions (i.e., expressing genuine anger) with the punitive action that violations of organizational norms entail? The crucial point is this: as a worker, one might get angry for the right moral reason; but there is simply no outlet for this expression (and the corrective action it signals) if the zone of expressive tolerance is next to nil.

As one explanation as to why the expressive zone of tolerance around anger can be so narrow, it is useful to consult Solomon (2003) again. He notes that our fear and foreboding of anger is so visceral that its mere display can prompt us to behave as if there is a real threat of harm behind it, even though we know that there is no such threat. Thus, workers may well end up in that awkward position and the consequences it entails when they have to suppress emotion, especially over issues that matter considerably to them (as suggested by Pennebaker, 1982).

Further to this, the motivation for the suppression is rooted in the sanctions that workers can potentially face if they dare express their anger. As Geddes and Callister (2007) note, both formal and informal sanctions can be imposed when workers' anger expressions cross the impropriety threshold. In terms of formal sanctions, these can be imposed by management (broadly conceived), and can range from changes in status or responsibility at work, to oral/written warn- ings, probation and suspension, to dismissal. However, Geddes and Callister (2007) argue that formal sanctions are more likely to emerge if a worker's expressed anger is perceived by higher status managers to have crossed the impropriety threshold. Informal sanctions can ensue when co-workers or management are unable or unwilling to formally sanction workers who express deviant anger. In such cases, they may nonetheless respond with informal sanctions against the worker, including in the form of obvious disapproval, avoidance, withdrawal, unflattering gossip and various disrespectful or aggressive behaviours (Geddes and Baron, 1997). No matter whether the sanctions that follow 'deviant' expressions of anger are formal or informal in kind, it should be understood that workers who openly express their anger (or other emotions) face an overwhelmingly intricate problem; expressing a truly felt emotion at work is a delicate act – it can help sustain or destabilize the social order (Fineman, 2001).

Despite the prospect of sanctions, as we have argued recently, the moral conviction to engage in corrective action may be strong enough for workers to accept a degree of personal risk following expressions of anger (Lindebaum and Geddes, 2016). Whether workers face immediate sanctions (e.g., losing their jobs) or whether the sanctions strengthen the workers' determination to explore professional alternatives, the chain of thought could look like this:

- There is an urge to express anger about events at work that are of abominable (i.e., morally repulsive) character.
- The urge to speak out is stronger than the fear of sanctions that would lead to the suppression of anger.
- This, in turn, can prompt workers to accept the risk inherent in speaking out (i.e., that they will face sanctions at work).

Depending upon whether they face immediate job losses (an external force) or whether the sanctions strengthen the worker's resolve to change jobs (an internal force) once viable alternatives manifest themselves, it is at this juncture that I propose we can speak of 'situation selection' as an antecedent-focused emotion regulation strategy to offer a solution to emotional repression at work.

3.3   SUMMARY

In this chapter, I have scrutinized the theoretical and empirical findings associated with Gross's widely used process model of emotion regulation (e.g., 1998, 2013). Building upon this, I have then explored specific emotion regulation strategies in order to show how they differentially apply to and impact upon the two pathways to social control introduced earlier in this book, giving detailed attention to each of the four focal emotions. In particular, through detailed description and illustration (see Figure 3.2), I have laid out for each emotion (shame, guilt, happiness and anger) what the current appraisal might look like, which, in turn, gives rise to a host of adverse psychological, physiological and social consequences. This was followed by suggestions as to how emotion might be regulated differently (compared to the status quo) to alleviate these adverse consequences. The emotion regulation strategy identified in relation to shame and guilt was reappraisal (and the associated tactic of psychological distancing), while I have advocated the genuine expression of emotion in response to these genuine emotions being suppressed in the context of happiness and anger.

Recognizing the risks associated with genuine expressions of emotion at work such as role conflict (as indicated in Figure 3.2) or destabilizing the order at work (see Fineman, 2001), I have refrained from predicting what the 'new' consequences for workers might be – other than suggesting that there will be a lower likelihood of adverse consequences materializing if they adopted these suggestions. This is entirely consistent with the aim in this book: to allow workers (or readers of this book) to explore what new consequences might be experienced instead through their own sense-making, creativity, spontaneity and need for autonomy. After all, to suggest that a particular consequence is less likely to occur is very different from stipulating what workers might experience instead. In Chapter 4, I will elaborate upon this further.

NOTES

1. Despite the focus on emotion regulation as an intrapersonal phenomenon (i.e., the within-person level analysis), our response tendencies are nonetheless inextricably linked to the social context, as classical investigations of authority and conformity (Asch, 1956; Milgram, 1974) as well as recent advances in emotion research (Lindebaum and Gabriel, 2016; Van Kleef, 2014) underline.
2. In fact, it can be sometimes difficult, from a practical real-life perspective, to distinguish each strategy sharply (e.g. situation selection vs. situation modification). Likewise, it is indeed possible that emotion regulation can also occur at multiple points and in parallel during the emotion-generative process (Gross and Thompson, 2007). However, while I recognize that these are crucial possibilities for future research, a detailed treatment of these possibilities is outside the purview of this book.
3. The prominence of this strategy in relation to the emancipatory journey of workers is made visible in full in Chapter 4.
4. These tactics have been described as: (a) explicitly positive, (b) change current circumstances, (c) reality challenge, (d) change future consequences, (e) agency, (f) distancing, (g) technical and (h) acceptance. They are included in the appendix of the article by McRae et al. (2012).
5. Note that expressive suppression forms also the theoretical mainstay in relation to Pathway II, when the expression of anger is responded to with informal or formal sanctions (Geddes and Callister, 2007), the fear of which prompts the suppression of emotion.
6. I will explain what I mean by 'reasonable boundaries' in a subsequent section.
7. As a side comment, it is worth noting that in this day and age, when 'teams' become the production unit as opposed to single workers (Osterman et al., 2001), it may in practice prove intractable to identify – beyond any doubt – that one specific situation caused by one specific worker led to the failure to meet performance expectations.
8. I personally welcome these propositions, but I wonder whether there is not an in-built contradiction in the arguments by Grandey and colleagues when they posit,

on the one hand, that there should be a ban on formalized emotion display at work (altogether?). On the other hand, they suggest that 'humanistic forms of emotional labor can also engage in fair policies that recognize and support the effort that is required by emotional labor' (Grandey et al., 2015, p. 780) and that organizations can communicate rewards for emotional effort. Why should we care or consider the latter two options if it is the principles behind them that are questioned?

9.   I note that the notion of emotionologies, though originating in historical studies on emotion, and more latterly applied in embryonic doses in management (Fineman, 2008), has still not received the attention it deserves among management researchers. Perhaps there might be a translational issue here: emotionologies represent a cultural variable (Stearns and Stearns, 1985) which, in turn, can have a bearing on the formation of individual attitudes and values (Tamir et al., 2016).

REFERENCES

Alvesson, M., and Willmott, H. (1992). On the idea of emancipation in management and organization studies. *Academy of Management Review*, **17**(3), 432–464.

Appleton, A. A., Buka, S. L., Loucks, E. B., Gilman, S. E., and Kubzansky, L. D. (2013). Divergent associations of adaptive and maladaptive emotion regulation strategies with inflammation. *Health Psychology: Official Journal of the Division of Health Psychology, American Psychological Association*, **32**(7), 748–756.

Asch, S. (1956). Studies of independence and conformity: I: a minority of one against a unanimous majority. *Psychological Monographs*, **70**(9), 1–70.

Barling, J., Dupré, K. E., and Kelloway, E. K. (2008). Predicting workplace aggression and violence. *Annual Review of Psychology*, **60**(1), 671–692.

Batson, C. D., Kennedy, C. L., Nord, L.-A., Stocks, E. L., Fleming, D. Y. A., Marzette, C. M., Lishner, D. A., Hayes, R. E., Kolchinsky, L. M., and Zerger, T. (2007). Anger at unfairness: is it moral outrage? *European Journal of Social Psychology*, **37**(6), 1272–1285.

Baumeister, R. F., Muraven, M., and Tice, D. M. (2000). Ego depletion: a resource model of volition, self-regulation, and controlled processing. *Social Cognition*, **18**(2), 130–150.

Bechara, A., Damasio, H., and Damasio, A. R. (2000). Emotion, decision making and the orbitofrontal cortex. *Cerebral Cortex*, **10**(3), 295–307.

Brotheridge, C. M., and Lee, R. T. (2003). Development and validation of the emotional labour scale. *Journal of Occupational and Organizational Psychology*, **76**(3), 365–379.

Buhle, J. T., Silvers, J. A., Wager, T. D., Lopez, R., Onyemekwu, C., Kober, H., Weber, K., and Ochsner, K. N. (2014). Cognitive reappraisal of emotion: a meta-analysis of human neuroimaging studies. *Cerebral Cortex*, **24**(11), 2981–2990.

Butler, E. A., Egloff, B., Wilhelm, F. H., Smith, N. C., Erickson, E. A., and Gross, J. J. (2003). The social consequences of expressive suppression. *Emotion*, **3**(1), 48–67.

Butler, E. A., and Gross, J. J. (2009). Emotion and emotion regulation: integrating individual and social levels of analysis. *Emotion Review*, **1**(1), 86–87.

Chang, M.-L. (2009). An appraisal perspective of teacher burnout: examining the emotional work of teachers. *Educational Psychology Review*, **21**(3), 193–218.

Connerton, P. (ed.) (1976). *Critical Sociology*. Harmondsworth, UK: Penguin.

Creed, W. E. D., Hudson, B. A., Okhuysen, G. A., and Smith-Crowe, K. (2014). Swimming in a sea of shame: incorporating emotion into explanations of institutional reproduction and change. *Academy of Management Review*, **39**(3), 275–301.

Denny, B. T., and Ochsner, K. N. (2014). Behavioral effects of longitudinal training in cognitive reappraisal. *Emotion*, **14**(2), 425–433.

Diefendorff, J. M., Richard, E. M., and Yang, J. (2008). Linking emotion regulation strategies to affective events and negative emotions at work. *Journal of Vocational Behavior*, **73**(3), 498–508.

Domagalski, T. A., and Steelman, L. A. (2005). The impact of work events and disposition on the experience and expression of employee anger. *Organizational Analysis*, **13**(1), 31–52.

Fineman, S. (2001). Emotions and organizational control. In R. Payne and C. L. Cooper (eds), *Emotions at Work: Theory, Research and Applications for Management* (pp. 219–240). Chichester: Wiley.

Fineman, S. (2003). *Understanding Emotion at Work*. London: Sage.

Fineman, S. (ed.) (1993). *Emotion in Organizations*. London: Sage.

Fineman, S. (ed.) (2008). *The Emotional Organization*. Oxford: Blackwell.

Flynn, F. J., and Schaumberg, R. L. (2012). When feeling bad leads to feeling good: guilt-proneness and affective organizational commitment. *Journal of Applied Psychology*, **97**(1), 124–133.

Frijda, N. (2013). Emotion regulation: two souls in one breast? In D. Hermans, B. Rimé, and B. Mesquita (eds), *Changing Emotions* (pp. 137–143). Hove, UK: Psychology Press.

Geddes, D., and Baron, R. A. (1997). Workplace aggression as a consequence of negative performance feedback. *Management Communication Quarterly*, **10**(4), 433–454.

Geddes, D., and Callister, R. R. (2007). Crossing the line(s): a dual threshold model of anger in organizations. *Academy of Management Review*, **32**(3), 721–746.

Geddes, D., and Callister, R. R. (2014). Message in the madness: finding value in anger expressions at work. Paper presented at the Academy of Management meeting in Philadelphia, 1–5 August.

Geddes, D., and Lindebaum, D. (forthcoming). Strategic expressions of emotions at work.

Gibson, D. E., and Callister, R. R. (2010). Anger in organizations: review and integration. *Journal of Management*, **36**(1), 66–93.

Graesser, A. C., Woll, S. B., Kowalski, D. J., and Smith, D. A. (1980). Memory for typical and atypical actions in scripted activities. *Journal of Experimental Psychology: Human Learning and Memory*, **6**(5), 503–515.

Grandey, A. A. (2000). Emotion regulation in the workplace: a new way to conceptualize emotional labor. *Journal of Occupational Health Psychology*, **5**(1), 95–110.

Grandey, A. A., and Gabriel, A. S. (2015). Emotional labor at a crossroads: where do we go from here? *Annual Review of Organizational Psychology and Organizational Behavior*, **2**(1), 323–349.

Grandey, A. A., Rupp, D., and Brice, W. N. (2015). Emotional labor threatens decent work: a proposal to eradicate emotional display rules. *Journal of Organizational Behavior*, **36**(6), 770–785.

Gross, J. J. (1998). The emerging field of emotion regulation: an integrative review. *Review of General Psychology*, **2**(3), 271–299.

Gross, J. J. (2002). Emotion regulation: affective, cognitive, and social consequences. *Psychophysiology*, **39**(3), 281–291.

Gross, J. J. (2013). Emotion regulation: taking stock and moving forward. *Emotion*, **13**(3), 359–365.

Gross, J. J., and John, O. P. (2003). Individual differences in two emotion regulation processes: implications for affect, relationships, and well-being. *Journal of Personality and Social Psychology*, **85**(2), 348–362.

Gross, J. J., and Levenson, R. W. (1997). Hiding feelings: the acute effects of inhibiting negative and positive emotion. *Journal of Abnormal Psychology*, **106**(1), 95–103.

Gross, J. J., Richards, J. M., and John, O. P. (2006). Emotion regulation in everyday life. In D. K. Snyder, J. A. Simpson, and J. N. Hughes (eds), *Emotion Regulation in Families: Pathways to Dysfunction and Health* (pp. 13–35). Washington, DC: American Psychological Association.

Gross, J. J., and Thompson, R. D. (2007). Emotion regulation: conceptual foundations. In J. Gross (ed.), *Handbook of Emotion Regulation* (pp. 3–24). New York: Guilford Press.

Henderson, M., Brooks, S. K., del Busso, L., Chalder, T., Harvey, S. B., Hotopf, M., Madan, I., and Hatch, S. (2012). Shame! Self-stigmatisation as an obstacle to sick doctors returning to work: a qualitative study. *BMJ Open*, **2**(5).

Hochschild, A. R. (1979). Emotion work, feeling rules and social structure. *American Journal of Sociology*, **85**(3), 551–575.

John, O. P., and Gross, J. J. (2004). Healthy and unhealthy emotion regulation: personality processes, individual differences, and life span development. *Journal of Personality*, **72**(6), 1301–1334.

Jordan, P. J., and Lindebaum, D. (2015). A model of within person variation in leadership: emotion regulation and scripts as predictors of situationally appropriate leadership. *Leadership Quarterly*, **26**(4), 594–605.

Kahneman, D. (2000). Experienced utility and objective happiness: a moment-based approach. In D. Kahneman and A. Tversky (eds), *Choices, Values and Frames* (pp. 673–692). Cambridge: Cambridge University Press.

Kiffin-Petersen, S., and Murphy, S. (2016). Ashamed of being ashamed: talk-inhibiting, soul-stifling feelings of shame. Paper presented at the 10th EMONET Conference in Rome, 3–4 July.

Kim, S., Thibodeau, R., and Jorgensen, R. S. (2011). Shame, guilt, and depressive symptoms: a meta-analytic review. *Psychological Bulletin*, **137**(1), 68–96.

Lawrence, S. A., Troth, A. C., Jordan, P. J., and Collins, A. L. (2011). A review of emotion regulation and development of a framework for emotion regulation in the workplace. In P. L. Perrewe and D. C. Ganster (eds), *Research in Occupational Stress and Well-Being: The Role of Individual Differences in Occupational Stress and Well-Being* (Vol. 9, pp. 199–266). London: Emerald.

Lindebaum, D. (2012). I rebel – therefore we exist: emotional standardization in organizations and the emotionally intelligent individual. *Journal of Management Inquiry*, **21**(3), 262–277.

Lindebaum, D. (2015). A qualitative study of emotional intelligence and its underlying processes and outcomes in management studies. In C. E. J. Härtel, W. J. Zerbe, and N. M. Ashkanasy (eds), *New Ways of Studying Emotion in Organizations: Research on Emotion in Organizations* (Vol. 11, pp. 109–137). Bingley, UK: Emerald.

Lindebaum, D., and Gabriel, Y. (2016). Anger and organization studies: from social disorder to moral order. *Organization Studies*, **37**(7), 903–918.

Lindebaum, D., and Geddes, D. (2016). The place and role of (moral) anger in organizational behavior studies. *Journal of Organizational Behavior*, **37**(5), 738–757.

Lindebaum, D., Jordan, P. J., and Morris, L. (2016). Symmetrical and asymmetrical outcomes of leader anger expression: a qualitative study of army personnel. *Human Relations*, **69**(2), 277–300.

Lyubomirsky, S., King, L., and Diener, E. (2005). The benefits of frequent positive affect: does happiness lead to success? *Psychological Bulletin*, **131**(6), 803–855.

Mason, P. (2015). Politicians love dressing up in hi-vis vests, but they ignore what's really happening to modern workers. *The Guardian*, 12 April.

Masters, J. C. (1991). Strategies and mechanisms for the personal and social control of emotion. In J. Garber and K. A. Dodge (eds), *The Development of Emotion Regulation and Dysregulation* (pp. 182–207). New York: Cambridge University Press.

McRae, K., Ciesielski, B., and Gross, J. J. (2012). Unpacking cognitive reappraisal: goals, tactics, and outcomes. *Emotion*, **12**(2), 250–255.

Milgram, S. (1974). *Obedience to Authority*. New York: Harper & Row.

Mill, J. S. (1861/2001). *Utilitarianism*. London: Electric Book Co.

Montada, L., and Schneider, A. (1989). Justice and emotional reactions to the disadvantaged. *Social Justice Research*, **3**(4), 313–344.

Noah, T. (2013). Labor of love: the enforced happiness of Pret A Manger. *New Republic*. Retrieved from https://newrepublic.com/article/112204/pret-manger-when-corporations-enforce-happiness on 12 June 2016.

O'Mara, E. M., Jackson, L. E., Batson, C. D., and Gaertner, L. (2011). Will moral outrage stand up? Distinguishing among emotional reactions to a moral violation. *European Journal of Social Psychology*, **41**(2), 173–179.

Osterman, P., Kochan, T. A., Locke, R., and Piore, M. J. (2001). *Working in America: A Blueprint for the New Labor Market*. Cambridge, MA: MIT Press.

106 *Emancipation through emotion regulation at work*

Pennebaker, J. W. (1982). *Opening Up: The Healing Power of Confiding in Others*. New York: William Morrow and Company.
Scherer, K. R., Schorr, A., and Johnstone, T. E. (eds) (2001). *Appraisal Processes in Emotion: Theory, Methods, Research*. New York: Oxford University Press.
Scott, C., and Myers, K. K. (2005). The socialization of emotion: learning emotion management at the fire station. *Journal of Applied Communication Research*, **33**(1), 67–92.
Sheppes, G., Scheibe, S., Suri, G., and Gross, J. J. (2011). Emotion-regulation choice. *Psychological Science*, **22**(11), 1391–1396.
Smith, A. C., and Kleinman, S. (1989). Managing emotions in medical school: students' contacts with the living and the dead. *Social Psychology Quarterly*, **52**(1), 56–69.
Solomon, R. (2003). *Not Passion's Slave: Emotions and Choice*. Oxford: Oxford University Press.
Stearns, C. Z., and Stearns, P. N. (1986). *Anger: The Struggle for Emotional Control in America's Society*. Chicago: Chicago University Press.
Stearns, P. N., and Stearns, C. Z. (1985). Emotionology: clarifying the history of emotions and emotional standards. *American Historical Review*, **90**, 813–816.
Sutton, R. I. (1991). Maintaining norms about expressed emotions: the case of bill collectors. *Administrative Science Quarterly*, **36**(2), 245–268.
Tamir, M., Schwartz, S. H., Cieciuch, J., Riediger, M., Torres, C., Scollon, C., Dzokoto, V., Zhou, X., and Vishkin, A. (2016). Desired emotions across cultures: a value-based account. *Journal of Personality and Social Psychology*, **111**(1), 67–82.
Tangney, J. P. (1990). Assessing individual differences in proneness to shame and guilt: development of the self-conscious affect and attribution inventory. *Journal of Personality and Social Psychology*, **59**(1), 102–111.
Tangney, J. P., Dearing, R. L., Wagner, P. E., and Gramzow, R. (2000). *The Test of Self-Conscious Affect-3 (TOSCA-3)*. Fairfax, VA: George Mason University.
Tavris, C. (1982). *Anger: The Misunderstood Emotion*. New York: Simon & Schuster.
Tracy, S. J., and Tracy, K. (1998). Emotion labor at 911: a case study and theoretical critique. *Journal of Applied Communication Research*, **26**(4), 390–411.
Van Kleef, G. A. (2014). Understanding the positive and negative effects of emotional expressions in organizations: EASI does it. *Human Relations*, **67**(9), 1145–1164.
Van Kleef, G. A., Homan, A. C., and Cheshin, A. (2012). Emotional influence at work: take it EASI. *Organizational Psychology Review*, **2**(4), 311–339.

4. Conclusion

This book set out to advocate the idea of *emancipating emotion at work* by enabling workers to regulate their emotions *differently* toward that end vis-à-vis the emotional repression they experience. In this chapter, I shall offer a synthesis of the main arguments developed throughout the book. Before I attend to this task, however, I would like to offer two reminders. First, in its own particular way, the motivation behind this book was much more than simply being an academic monograph that hopefully convinces a few university libraries to procure it for their student or academic audience. Instead, any attempt at 'passionate' scholarship (Courpasson, 2013; Lindebaum and Gabriel, 2016), at least in my view, must go beyond standards of intellectual rigour and theoretical clarity and ensure that real-world and first-hand experiences, while adhering to these standards, must have political and social relevance. To this end, I have justified from the start the necessity to use essayistic prose to signal the interventionist intention behind this book. For this reason – and I hope the reader will bear with me (apologies, I couldn't bite back this temptation) – that I draw this book to a close with a special personal task. Second, as I have readily admitted in Chapter 1, I wrote this book with a view to opening up the conversation around emancipating emotions – as opposed to settling or containing the issue.

Although I went to some length to articulate the conceptual boundaries of this book in Chapter 1, I recognize that I have not covered all angles within the key literatures discussed. Neither do I claim to have identified all adjacent topics of potential theoretical relevance in this book. This is fine by me (at least it does not cause me sleepless nights), for there is only so much a single book can aim for and accomplish. What I humbly hope, however, is that the ideas presented herein stimulate future research as well as wider societal and policy debates around contemporary work practices.

4.1   SYNTHESIS

In order to flesh out the processes implicated in the transition from an un-emancipated to an emancipated existence, and how they build upon and connect with each other, I have traversed several key literatures in this book. To begin with, I have devoted particular attention to critical theory and its inherent aim to emancipate or, in other words, to liberate workers from repressive conditions at work. Given that it is emotion that constitutes this repressive condition, a fruitful angle emerged in which critical theory and the literature on emotion regulation could mutually – and in quite advantageous ways – inform each other.

For one thing, I have proposed that emotion regulation can be one potential mechanism through which emancipation of workers can be achieved, bearing in mind that traditional confines of critical theorizing (i.e., an over-appreciation of structural and relational concerns denying workers any agentic impulses) may not, strictly speaking, enable the emancipation of workers. Therefore, structural and relational concerns need to be relaxed in order to allow workers to act in agentic, self-efficacious and self-determining ways. I have supported this contention with reference to Bandura's (1977, 1997) work on self-efficacy and its consequences, as well as with the life accomplishments of Rupert Neudeck and his humanitarian organization, Cap Anamur.

For another, I have speculated that we can gain a better and deeper understanding of emotion regulation if we were to appreciate emancipation as one (but not exclusive) moral endpoint as to why we regulate emotion. This seems plausible, for the act of self-regulating one's emotion is directed toward desired end states, and these also refer to phenomenological states indicating affective contents (Tamir et al., 2016).

To elaborate further, Frijda (2013) concludes that 'the motivations for emotion regulation are themselves emotional. They are often as emotional as the regulated emotion itself . . . Emotions are regulated to the extent that one cares about the implications of having an unregulated emotion' (p. 139). Applied to the context of this book, workers may care – for their own benefit – about regulating their emotions differently in the case of shame and guilt, while in relation to happiness and anger, they may actually care to experience unregulated emotion (i.e., the need for suppression is removed). This appears reasonable to advocate, since the ultimate end of emancipation is to enable workers in society to modify their lives by nurturing in them a sense of understanding and self-knowledge of their social conditions which can then function as the foundation for such modification (Fay, 1987). There is, thus, a distinct teleological implication here that goes far beyond generic and abstract references to 'goals' in the emotion regulatory process (Gross, 1998; Gross and Thompson, 2007).

Drawing upon emotion research more generally, and social functional accounts of emotion more specifically, enabled me then to articulate two pathways to social control from which workers could emancipate themselves (assuming that this book can be one catalyst to this end). Figure 4.1 seeks to illustrate the key premises and stages of the emancipatory journey of workers. I note, importantly, that Figure 4.1 does not represent a 'model' in the hypothetico-deductive sense, setting out propositions for empirical testing. Instead, it should be considered as an organizing framework to synthesize the contents of the preceding chapters.

To begin with, Pathway I was based upon the observation that social functions of emotion are excessively exploited for organizational ends (e.g., in terms of performance increments or as tools of organizational control). This development is fanned by the presence of context-specific emotion norms and display rules at work (Diefendorff and Greguras, 2009; Lindebaum et al., 2016), as indicated in Figure 4.1.

Though by no means a final list, in this book I have exclusively examined shame, guilt and happiness within the scope of Pathway I. But there is a noteworthy feature of Pathway I, for while all three emotions are necessarily subsumed under the banner of 'excessive exploitation of functions', the approach to emotion regulation in a different way towards worker emancipation eventually requires that shame and guilt receive distinct treatment compared to happiness. This is because, as explained in Chapter 3, the effects of both shame and guilt can be mitigated by way of reappraising the situation via psychological distancing, while the same process does not hold for happiness. Underlying this is the fact that thought processes around shame and guilt, while dependent upon social cues, are oftentimes internalized processes over which workers may or may not have control (Henderson et al., 2012; Kiffin-Petersen and Murphy, 2016). By contrast, the expectation to smile, display a friendly demeanour

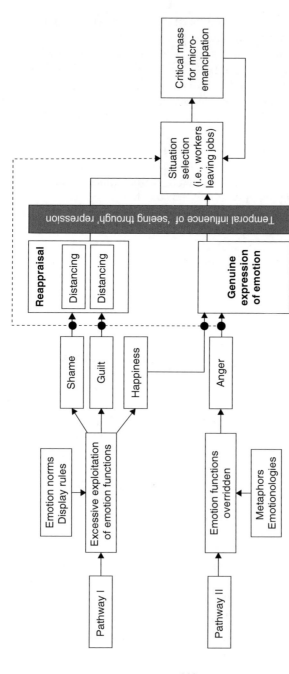

Note: Not a model in the deductive sense, setting out propositions for empirical testing. For now, it is an organizing framework to synthe-size the contents of the preceding chapters. The emotions are not 'outcomes', but conditions that are the subject of scrutiny here.

Figure 4.1   Pathways to social control, different approaches to emotion regulation and emancipation of workers

110

and be radiant in one's appearance when serving customers are externally imposed constraints (Grandey and Gabriel, 2015; Illouz, 2007). Therefore, in the context of Pathway I, happiness is not linked to the 'reappraisal' box, but instead connects to the 'genuine expression of emotion' box in Figure 4.1.

By contrast, Pathway II reflects the observation that the 'talk about anger' (as influenced by metaphors and emotionologies about it) overrides its very (and vital) social function – namely, to redress injustice. More explicitly, because the expression of anger at work, or generally in the public domain, is increasingly less tolerated due to lay and scholarly perceptions that it is a 'negative' emotion related to a host of 'negative' outcomes (but see Solomon, 2003; Solomon and Stone, 2002, for a powerful argument 'against valence'), and because these perceptions may not always differentiate accurately between 'anger expression', 'verbal abuse' or 'aggression' (at least in the UK; see Lindebaum and Geddes, 2016), the sanctions put in place to prevent these negative outcomes from occurring, in turn, lead to the suppression of anger on the part of workers in situations where the zone of expressive tolerance is highly compressed.

Crucially, the boxes in Figure 4.1 featuring the four focal emotions (shame, guilt, happiness and anger) do not constitute outcomes in the traditional sense. Rather, they represent conditions that are the subject of scrutiny here: in the case of shame and guilt, they represent a 'false consciousness' from which workers require liberation through emancipation (Geuss, 1981). That is, they reflect an existence in which workers have not yet seen through the power relations at work, how emotions are used in this process and what the consequences are for them. In contrast, the issue with anger is not that it represents a false consciousness, but rather that it signifies largely genuine consciousness in a suppressed condition. I use the word 'largely' in the preceding sentence to indicate that most workers will probably be aware that they face external impositions on what emotion displays are required by them (in the case of happiness) or which ones are prohibited (in the case of anger). The vignettes in Chapter 2 accompanying each of these emotions are also sensitive to this point.

Bearing this in mind, the model then relates these to specific emotion regulation approaches to alleviate the suffering associated with both states of undesirable consciousness. However, I propose that there are two potential pathways available to workers.

Whether workers select one over the other is contingent upon the (un)feasibility for them to quit their jobs and commence employment elsewhere. Thus, looking at Figure 4.1, the dotted line indicates the possibility to circumvent internal thought processes associated with emotion regulation and move straight to situation selection so that workers can remove themselves from the emotional repression experienced in their current place of work. That is, workers have the possibility to leave their jobs and have already secured, or are in the process of securing, alternative employment.

This applies to all emotions of interest here (as indicated by the nodes on the dotted line), although, as noted earlier, the motivation for such efforts is dissimilar in the case of shame and guilt compared to happiness and anger. With regard to shame and guilt, the deleterious effects upon workers caused by illegitimate and unwarranted attributions of responsibilities and causes of failures can – once they have seen through how current arrangements disadvantage them – prompt workers to change their external situation by leaving their jobs and commencing employment elsewhere.

In the case of happiness and anger, the motivation resides in the circumstance that workers – again once they have seen through how current arrangements disadvantage them – no longer wish to accept the consequences of emotion suppression (as outlined in Chapter 3). However, the act of suppressing emotion is motivated by different factors. In terms of happiness, workers are required to smile by virtue of display rules, even though they may not feel happy (e.g., when they feel angry about a rude customer), whereas workers might experience anger but are not permitted to express it by virtue of emotionologies and general metaphors around anger (cf. the case of Thomas in Vignette 2.4).

As noted before, while situation selection is also an antecedent-focused emotion regulation strategy (like cognitive change), this approach seeks to change the external environment (i.e., seeking a new job) so as to alter the emotional impact of events. In the absence of this option (and I appreciate that this might be the case for many workers), workers have the choice of engaging in reappraising the situation (via psychological distancing) in relation to shame and guilt or venturing to disobey display rules or emotionologies and express their genuinely felt emotions in terms of happiness and anger.

There are, of course, immediate risks surfacing for workers opting for genuine expressions of their emotions in the case of happiness and anger. After all, openly expressing emotion at work yields an intricate problem: expressing a truly felt emotion at work is a delicate act – it can help sustain or destabilize the social order (Fineman, 2001). Consequently, either workers would be perceived as not performing according to job descriptions (in the case of happiness) or as displaying 'deviant anger' (Geddes and Callister, 2007), both of which can potentially entail informal or formal sanctions such as peer pressure (Mason, 2015) or, in extreme cases, being made redundant.

Even though workers can pursue psychological distancing (regarding shame and guilt) or genuinely express emotion (regarding happiness and anger) as necessary adjustments to regulate their emotions in order to lessen the impact of emotional events upon them, the really acute and pressing question is for how long workers can accept and endure in the condition of emotional repression once they can see through the role of emotion as a means of repression. In consequence, the theorizing presented here has an unequivocal temporal dimension in cases where workers are unable to leave their jobs straight away in the face of emotional suffering. Of note, when I refer to the argument of leaving one's job straight away in the face of emotional suffering, I do not, needless to say, imply that there is one distinctively adverse event for workers. Instead, I want to be very clear that there is likely a trajectory of prior adverse experiences that have an accumulated effect over time. It is simply the latest event, then, that is the 'last straw' for workers to conclude 'That's it! Enough is enough. I'm out of here.' Thus, the model in Figure 4.1 reflects this temporal recognition by incorporating the grey box right next to the boxes concerning emotion regulation strategies.

Taken together, dissatisfaction with the status quo may prompt workers to alter their conditions both within and in relation to social structures. In terms of within-changes, I have elaborated at some length upon the role of reappraisal and genuine expression of emotion as ways to start establishing a psychological buffer for workers. However, in terms of altering social structures and practices, what I propose is this: if it is possible to prompt workers to increasingly opt for situation selection as a way to pre-empt the emotional suffering experienced in prior jobs, this will constitute a meaningful first step to further grow the critical mass of an emancipated workforce I have silhouetted here. A larger critical mass would indicate an acceleration of staff turnover within organizations or, better still, render turnover numbers unsustainable for organizations. The initiation of such critical mass and movement, in turn, may prompt other workers to decide to change their jobs, hence the feedback loop in Figure 4.1 from 'critical mass for micro-emancipation' to 'situation selection'. It may be then under such conditions that changes to the social structure and practices may become noticeable and necessary (perhaps in line with the suggestions offered by Grandey et al., 2015).

At the same time, I am mindful of the challenge articulated by Harry Holzer, who thinks that 'it is such a buyer's market in the labor market – because of so many unemployed workers per job – that employers can get away with a lot of demands on their workers that ordinarily wouldn't be possible' (cited in Noah, 2013). Further to this, in cases where markets are given priority for the allocation of jobs, workers are more likely to accept poor roles in conditions of undue economic constraint. In consequence, many workers have jobs not quite to their liking or choosing, or jobs that they find 'unworthy, uninteresting, underpaid [or] set in authoritarian working environments' (Blanc and Al-Amoudi, 2013, p. 514). Thus, the conditions for the disappearance (or at least reduction) of unworthy and unfulfilling jobs still need to be created (along the lines advocated above).

4.2   LOOKING AHEAD

Throughout this book, I have deliberately abstained from offering excessively prescriptive suggestions. What I have done – to put this in condensed form – is state that emancipation is the aim of this book, and offered emotion regulation as a tool to this end. What I have *not* done, however, is prescribe what and how workers might feel – in their own phenomenological world – as a result of having used insights from the emotion regulation literature to obtain an emancipated existence. As explicitly highlighted in Chapter 3, I have framed the 'new consequences' emerging as a result of regulating emotion differently simply as indicating a lower likelihood of adverse psychological physiological and social consequences afflicting workers in the future (see Figure 3.2).

So what, then, does the future hold for workers sensitive to the ideas presented here? My position is that the effects of emotion research generally, and its effects in the context of this book, often do not immediately manifest themselves. Instead, they rather develop over time as the insights are applied to, or judged against, current or even future real-life situations. It is then the iterative and cumulative interaction between the insights offered in this book and how workers continuously apply these to *their own* life histories and situations that will create an 'impact' over time. Consequently, it is key how we make sense of all this. Importantly, emotions are intimately entwined with our sense-making processes, because emotions both initiate and are the outcomes of sense-making (which literally means 'the making of sense' (Weick, 1995, p. 4). As he further noted:

> The reality of flows becomes most apparent when that flow is interrupted. An interruption to a flow typically induces an emotional response, which then paves the way for emotion to influence sensemaking. It is precisely because ongoing flows are subject to interruption that sensemaking is infused with feeling. (1995, p. 45)

While sensemaking is both retrospective and prospective, retrospective sensemaking nevertheless affects future sensemaking (Weick, 1995). Thus, sensemaking is 'ongoing in duration, having no single point of departure and no permanent point of arrival' (Dougherty and Drumheller, 2006, p. 217). Seen in this light, especially for emotion researchers, this implies that the effects of having once been exposed to the ideas presented here are largely unpredictable in terms of *when* an effect will occur and, more importantly, *how* the effect manifests itself in the phenomenological world of workers.

As I have appreciated consistently in this book, while some external and observable behaviours might be discernible on the part of workers (i.e., in terms of situation selection) en route to an emancipated existence, the intricacies and complexities of the phenomenological world of workers are too manifold to permit offering any predictions beyond situation selection. True to the spirit of critical theory, I contend that there are potentially fascinating insights to be unearthed in future research in terms of how the creativity, spontaneity and need for autonomy among workers aid in the reconfiguration and maintenance of (or perhaps even challenge to) their emancipated existence. Whether this is limited to the ideas presented in this book (especially in relation to situation selection) or whether the creativity, spontaneity and need for autonomy among workers yields entire unexpected results, I believe that there is ample opportunity for future research to engage with these ideas.

Of course, I offer this observation as someone largely steeped in the broader emotions at work literature. I agree with Gross (2013) that many other disciplines can meaningfully add to our substantive understanding of emotion regulation more generally, such as psychiatry, philosophy, sociology or business studies. However, to better understand the context sensitivity of the ideas developed here, I would add that the fields of micro-economics (with its interest in the behaviour of individuals and organizations in making decisions concerning the allocation of limited resources) and industrial relations (with its interest in the relations between management and workers in industry) can also bring highly germane insights to the discussion to facilitate the cross-fertilization among scientists across disciplines to gain a more complete understanding of the causes and consequences of emotion regulation. I hope that this cross-fertilization helps advance theoretically and empirically the ideas that I started to articulate in this book.

However, some critics might accuse me of indulging in wishful thinking as far as the idea is concerned that workers actually quit their current jobs based upon the ideas developed here and, more ludicrously still, that this can nurture the emergence of micro-emancipation among workers to such an extent that staff turnover becomes unsustainable for organizations. It will be the task of future research to empirically examine this proposition. It is then against the evidence produced that we can gauge the soundness of this idea. In the meantime, if the affirmation among critical theorists toward the potential for workers to act with creativity, spontaneity and autonomy bears any substance, then I believe that there is scope for this book to make a modest contribution to management research and, perhaps even more importantly, to management practice and the lives of workers. To invoke Durkheim (1893/2014) again, 'we should [not] give up the idea of improving [reality]' (p. 4). Nothing more needs to be said.

4.3 A PERSONAL TASK . . . *

* Early on I have emphasized the interventionist intention of this book. This blank space is designed to allow your imagination to ignite that intervention; it is not a whimsical way to draw the book to a close. If desired, you could apply the ideas to concrete situations at work, or more generally in interacting with others. Should you wish to share details of your emancipatory journey, I would be delighted to hear from you (mail@dirklindebaum.EU). Be assured that all information will be treated with strict confidentiality.

REFERENCES

Bandura, A. (1977). Self-efficacy: toward a unified theory of behavioral change. *Psychological Review*, **84**, 191–215.

Bandura, A. (1997). *Self-Efficacy: The Exercise of Control*. New York: Freeman.

Blanc, S., and Al-Amoudi, I. (2013). Corporate institutions in a weakened welfare state: a Rawlsian perspective. *Business Ethics Quarterly*, **23**(4), 497–525.

Courpasson, D. (2013). On the erosion of 'passionate scholarship'. *Organization Studies*, **34**(9), 1243–1249.

Diefendorff, J. M., and Greguras, G. J. (2009). Contextualizing emotional display rules: examining the roles of targets and discrete emotions in shaping display rule perceptions. *Journal of Management*, **35**(4), 880–898.

Dougherty, D. S., and Drumheller, K. (2006). Sensemaking and emotions in organizations: accounting for emotions in a rational(ized) context. *Communication Studies*, **57**(2), 215–238.

Durkheim, E. (1893/2014). *The Division of Labor in Society*. New York: Free Press.

Fay, B. (1987). *Critical Social Science*. Cambridge: Polity Press.

Fineman, S. (2001). Emotions and organizational control. In R. Payne and C. L. Cooper (eds), *Emotions at Work: Theory, Research and Applications for Management* (pp. 219–240). Chichester: Wiley.

Frijda, N. (2013). Emotion regulation: two souls in one breast? In D. Hermans, B. Rimé, and B. Mesquita (eds), *Changing Emotions* (pp. 137–143). Hove, UK: Psychology Press.

Geddes, D., and Callister, R. R. (2007). Crossing the line(s): A dual threshold model of anger in organizations. *Academy of Management Review*, **32**(3), 721–746.

Geuss, R. (1981). *The Idea of a Critical Theory: Habermas and the Frankfurt School*. Cambridge: Cambridge University Press.

Grandey, A. A., and Gabriel, A. S. (2015). Emotional labor at a crossroads: where do we go from here? *Annual Review of Organizational Psychology and Organizational Behavior*, **2**(1), 323–349.

Grandey, A. A., Rupp, D., and Brice, W. N. (2015). Emotional labor threatens decent work: a proposal to eradicate emotional display rules. *Journal of Organizational Behavior*, **36**(6), 770–785.

Gross, J. J. (1998). The emerging field of emotion regulation: an integrative review. *Review of General Psychology*, **2**(3), 271–299.

Gross, J. J. (2013). Emotion regulation: taking stock and moving forward. *Emotion*, **13**(3), 359–365.

Gross, J. J., and Thompson, R. D. (2007). Emotion regulation: conceptual foundations. In J. Gross (ed.), *Handbook of Emotion Regulation* (pp. 3–24). New York: Guilford Press.

Henderson, M., Brooks, S. K., del Busso, L., Chalder, T., Harvey, S. B., Hotopf,

M., Madan, I., and Hatch, S. (2012). Shame! Self-stigmatisation as an obstacle to sick doctors returning to work: a qualitative study. *BMJ Open*, **2**(5).

Illouz, E. (2007). *Cold Intimacies: The Making of Emotional Capitalism.* Cambridge: Polity.

Kiffin-Petersen, S., and Murphy, S. (2016). Ashamed of being ashamed: talk-inhibiting, soul-stifling feelings of shame. Paper presented at the 10th EMONET Conference in Rome, 3–4 July.

Lindebaum, D., and Gabriel, Y. (2016). Anger and organization studies: from social disorder to moral order. *Organization Studies*, **37**(7), 903–918.

Lindebaum, D., and Geddes, D. (2016). The place and role of (moral) anger in organizational behavior studies. *Journal of Organizational Behavior*, **37**(5), 738–757

Lindebaum, D., Jordan, P. J., and Morris, L. (2016). Symmetrical and asymmetrical outcomes of leader anger expression: a qualitative study of army personnel. *Human Relations*, **69**(2), 277–300.

Mason, P. (2015). Politicians love dressing up in hi-vis vests, but they ignore what's really happening to modern workers. *The Guardian*, 12 April.

Noah, T. (2013). Labor of love: the enforced happiness of Pret A Manger. *New Republic*. Retrieved from https://newrepublic.com/article/112204/pret-manger-when-corporations-enforce-happiness on 12 June 2016.

Solomon, R. (2003). *Not Passion's Slave: Emotions and Choice.* Oxford: Oxford University Press.

Solomon, R., and Stone, L. D. (2002). On 'positive' and 'negative' emotions. *Journal for the Theory of Social Behaviour*, **32**(4), 417–435.

Tamir, M., Schwartz, S. H., Cieciuch, J., Riediger, M., Torres, C., Scollon, C., Dzokoto, V., Zhou, X., and Vishkin, A. (2016). Desired emotions across cultures: a value-based account. *Journal of Personality and Social Psychology*, **111**(1), 67–82.

Weick, K. E. (1995). *Sensemaking in Organizations.* Thousand Oaks, CA: Sage.

Appendix

LINKING AUTOETHNOGRAPHY AND IDENTITY THEORY TO MAKE SENSE OF POWER ABUSES BY CABIN CREWS*

Background

'You are being aggressive ... I am not having this anymore' and, turning to another member of the cabin crew, the cabin manager added, 'Inform the captain that this passenger should be received by police on arrival.' This epiphany represents the climax of a dreadful experience we had (i.e., the two authors, a married couple) on a flight from Greece to the UK returning from our holidays in 2012 with our two young children (then aged nine months and three years). The tirade of threats was directed at one of us (the father), as we were both involved in a situation that had its roots in a confrontation between a fellow passenger (a 50+ quiet and friendly woman who sat behind us) and the cabin crew. A detailed description of the event can be found following this developmental paper in the form of a letter we sent to the airline (we loosely refer to the airline as the Orange-White Airline (OWA), just as we could refer to them as the Blue-White Airline).

As the letter indicates, at the heart of the situation was what we perceived to be a gross violation of what is measured, decent and fair treatment of others, especially if such acts are executed by individuals with formal power – i.e., the cabin manager has the power to initiate appropriate procedures to deal with disruptive passengers by requesting the pilot to get the police involved upon arrival, as the opening account suggests (see also Bor, 2007). We, therefore, concur with Scott (1992), who defines power as having access to resources. In that particular situation, the cabin crew had access to police when feeling threatened, but the passengers did not.

Upon reflection, it was the insistence on our ideals – such as fairness, acting on unfolding injustice or abuse of power and helping others when they cannot defend themselves – that led us to intervene and defend the fellow passenger against illegitimate accusations. In addition, the way things unfolded meant that we were then at the receiving end of power abuses, being threatened for simply questioning staff conduct towards fellow passengers.

But this sanitized and sterile description could just as well be put more plainly: we felt angry, very angry, which seems plausible given that anger is 'direct and explicit in its projection of our personal values and expectations on the world. Anger, whether expressed or not, is our insistence upon our own ideals . . . oneself as defender of values' (Solomon, 1993, pp. 227 and 229). We both have aversions against the characteristics of a 'postemotional society' (Mestrović, 1999). That is, individuals cease reacting to incidents that once caused natural turmoil and crisis – having become too blasé and too 'allergic' to getting involved while being intelligent enough to understand that these incidents are significant.

As we awaited our luggage at the carousel, the idea blurted out that our lived experience could be turned into an academic paper (at that stage it was said in jest). On further reflection, however, the moral conviction sank in that this *had to be* shared with the scholarly community. The standardized, evasive and dishonest response of the airline's customer services directly contradicting our account of the situation led to further frustration and the need to find some sort of moral resolution for this experience. This situation, we felt, should not be 'shrouded in secrecy' (Ellis and Bochner, 1996, p. 25) since it caused us significant distress at the time, probably an experience many other passengers also undergo with so-called budget air travel (see also Brown, 2006 for an interesting perspective). It is this distress that prompted us to embark (for the first time for both of us) upon an autoethnographic journey. Autoethnography has been defined as 'an autobiographical genre of writing that displays multiple layers of consciousness, connecting the personal to the cultural' (Ellis and Bochner, 2000, p. 733), and scholars have suggested that autoethnographic epiphanies often result from painful live experiences (Ellis and Bochner, 1996).

Method and Focus

In using autoethnography, our aim is both to be *analytical* and *evocative* in order 'to illuminate the relationship between the individual and the organization in a way that crystallizes the key conceptual and theoretical contributions to understanding the relationship between culture and organization' (Boyle and Parry, 2007, p. 185).

Analytically, one distinguishing feature of autoethnography is its focus on the self. As a result, one key debate pertains to the relationships between theories of the self or identity on the one hand, and methods of representing the self on the other (Learmonth and Humphreys, 2012). In consequence, we are sympathetic to Anderson's (2006, p. 392) concern 'for reclaiming and refining autoethnography as part of the analytical ethnographic tradition'. To ensure this analytic element, we draw upon identity theory (Hitlin, 2003; Hogg et al., 1995; Stryker and Burke, 2000) in the remainder of this paper. Identity theory is a micro-sociological theory that seeks to explain an individual's role-related behaviour. While it focuses on the reciprocal link between social structures and individual action, identity theory scholars have been most interested in individualistic outcomes of identity-related behaviours (Hogg et al., 1995).

Concepts like role-identity, identity salience, commitment to that identity, personal identity and its association with values feature prominently in this theory (Hitlin, 2003; Hogg et al., 1995; Stryker and Burke, 2000). Importantly, personal values often enter the stage in the presence of conflict. It is in the light of conflict that they enter our awareness and become guiding principles for our actions (Hitlin, 2003). In particular, we would like to explore how particular social structures (in this case involving a service setting combined with formal authority) influence, encourage or prohibit the enactment of identities (as customers, parents, academics) through an interplay with particular values (such as the need to react to injustice and power abuse, our duty to protect our children and so on). We could observe how the situation on board prohibited certain passengers from reacting, while for us the situation provided an unrelenting urge to speak out.

Whilst the literature has been extensively concerned with issues of customer abuse towards service staff (Bishop and Hoel, 2008; Boyd, 2002), avoiding disruptive passenger behaviours and making them comply with instructions issued to ensure health and safety requirements (Bor, 2007), disproportionate uses of power on the part of cabin crews are rarely acknowledged in the organizational or sociological literature. This is also reflected in organizational practices: when most airlines clearly delineate in their 'terms and conditions' what is acceptable passenger behaviour in the aircraft and the rights of staff, there is very little, if any, reference to acceptable standards of staff behaviour.

At the same time, we deem it central to draw out the evocative powers of autoethnography since, like many other caring social scientists, we 'want to change the world by writing from the heart' (Denzin, 2006, p. 422), though we apply a more humble interpretation here of Denzin's injunction. Given the nature of our experience, we are keen to expose the reader to this episode that would otherwise probably remain undetected and hidden to scholarly inquiry, be it that the method itself cannot reveal it or that access to appropriate research sites would not be granted (just imagine an airline's response to a request to examine power abuse by cabin crews). It is far too important to bring this episode to the attention of social science researcher so as to initiate debate, empirical consideration and ultimately hard thinking about organizational practice and how this affects both cabin crews and passengers. More generally speaking, this incident proffers meaningful revelations about wider political organizational agendas and practices in relation to airline safety. These, we should state, often include the imperative to make passengers comply with instructions issued so as to ensure health and safety requirements on board. In addition, we should highlight that, although our experience is rooted in the airline industry, we can detect very similar patterns in other organizational contexts, such as hospitals.

NOTE

* This appendix features a paper that was previously presented at a conference. The full reference is: Raftopoulou, C. E, and Lindebaum, D. (2013). Linking autoethnography and identity theory to make sense of power abuses by cabin crews. Paper presented at the British Academy of Management Conference in Liverpool, UK, 10–12 September.

REFERENCES

Anderson, L. (2006). Analytic autoethnography. *Journal of Contemporary Ethnography*, **35**(4), 373–395.
Bishop, V., and Hoel, H. (2008). The customer is always right? Exploring the

concept of customer bullying in the British Employment Service. *Journal of Consumer Culture*, **8**(3), 341–367.

Bor, R. (2007). Psychological factors in airline passenger and crew behaviour: a clinical overview. *Travel Medicine and Infectious Disease*, **5**(4), 207–216.

Boyd, C. (2002). Customer violence and employee health and safety. *Work, Employment and Society*, **16**(1), 151–169.

Boyle, M., and Parry, K. (2007). Telling the whole story: the case for organizational autoethnography. *Culture and Organization*, **13**(3), 185–190.

Brown, S. (2006). Ambi-brand culture: on a wing and a swear with Ryanair. In J. Schroeder and M. Salzer-Mörling (eds), *Brand Culture* (pp. 50–66). London: Routledge.

Denzin, N. K. (2006). Analytic autoethnography, or déjà vu all over again. *Journal of Contemporary Ethnography*, **35**(4), 419–428.

Ellis, C., and Bochner, A. P. (1996). *Composing Ethnography: Alternative Forms of Qualitative Writing*. Walnut Creek, CA: Sage.

Ellis, C., and Bochner, A. P. (2000). Autoethnography, personal narrative, reflexivity. In N. Denzin and Y. Lincoln (eds), *Handbook of Qualitative Research* (pp. 733–768). Thousand Oaks, CA: Sage.

Hitlin, S. (2003). Values as the core of personal identity: drawing links between two theories of self. *Social Psychology Quarterly*, **66**(2), 118–137.

Hogg, M. A., Terry, D. J., and White, K. M. (1995). A tale of two theories: a critical comparison of identity theory with social identity theory. *Social Psychology Quarterly*, **58**(4), 255–269.

Learmonth, M., and Humphreys, M. (2012). Autoethnography and academic identity: glimpsing business school doppelgängers. *Organization*, **19**(1), 99–117.

Mestrović, S. G. (1999). *Postemotional Society*. London: Sage.

Scott, W. R. (1992). *Organizations: Rational, Natural and Open Systems*. Englewood Cliffs, NJ: Prentice Hall.

Solomon, R. (1993). *The Passions: Emotions and the Meaning of Life*. Indianapolis: Hackett.

Stryker, S., and Burke, P. J. (2000). The past, present, and future of an identity theory. *Social Psychology Quarterly*, **63**(4), 284–297.

THE LETTER

Below we detail the letter that was sent to OWA in response to our experience. We emphasize that, at the stage of writing this letter, we did not only seek an unreserved apology, but wrote the letter also as a data-generating exercise, having made up our minds to seriously do something about the treatment we experienced on the flight. For the sake of keeping this appendix as succinct as possible, we have refrained from including OWA's response. Suffice it to say that they did not respond to any specific question directly and specifically. When we re-sent the letter with a request for answers to our questions, customer services, in an act of fathomless imagination, sent the *same* [nothing-saying] response again.

Dear XXXXXX,

We are writing this letter to seek OWA's response to a number of incidents that I and my wife witnessed during the flight that took place on [date withheld intentionally] from Greece to the UK.

To explain, it happened that during the flight considerable amounts of waste started to litter the corridor. Note that we had not been provided with litter bags in the front pockets of the seats. Whilst members of staff passed by several times, they did not pick up any litter so at some point I was forced to collect some in a plastic bag that we brought ourselves.

At some point, a female passenger behind us asked members of staff to remove the rubbish. They refused on the basis that they were serving customers and could not do it for health and safety reasons. The lady then complained that the rubbish was there for almost an hour and she was not happy to stay with it for longer. The air hostess told her that she could dispose of the rubbish herself in the lavatory. The passenger got up with the rubbish and squeezed past a member of the cabin crew in the corridor to go to the toilet.

> – *Can you please explain OWA's health and safety policy in relation to this incident and how can OWA maintain basic hygiene standards during a flight if rubbish is left in corridors for up to an hour?*

A few moments later, the cabin manager 'Emma' [we use a pseudonym here] approached the lady passenger behind us. Without explaining the rationale for her demand, 'Emma' asked the lady for her booking reference and passport. On prompting by the lady as to why she demanded this information, 'Emma' replied: 'because you have been rude to a colleague of mine by pushing her to the side' en route to the toilet.

> – *Can you explain what are the rights of the passenger in this situation? Do they have to provide their personal information without any rationale provided?*

It is at this juncture that I [i.e., the father] got involved, as I did not witness this version of events and I believe that the cabin crew behaviour was rather intimating towards the passenger. I asked in a calm manner the crew manager 'Emma' how she defines rude in order to understand what her rationale was and she replied 'This is what I define as rude'. She then referred to OWA's 'zero tolerance policy' without being able to link the policy to the incident that took place.

> – *Can you explain OWA's 'zero tolerance policy' in relation to this situation? How do you define 'rudeness' and 'pushing' in this policy? (Clearly during this incident we, as witnesses, had completely different perceptions of what happened to staff members, otherwise we would not have been involved). How do you ensure that this policy is not used by staff members to prevent customers from complaining?*

At that point, as the discussion with her was rather futile, I (and other passengers) asked for a complaint form to document the needlessly escalating behaviour of the crew manager and one of her female colleagues (blond hair, black glasses – no name provided). Several requests were merely responded to by saying 'Can we discuss this in the galley?'

> – *Are OWA staff members not obliged to provide their names at a customer's request? Is it standard OWA policy that staff members do not provide complaint forms but summon customers to the galley instead?*

In the galley, Emma asked for my booking reference. Being surprised by her unaccountable request, she responded that I have become involved in the situation and need to provide the booking reference too. I pulled out the boarding passes for me and my family to see which one contains the booking reference (one had the labels for the luggage attached to it, but I could not see instantly which of one it was). Before I could find the right pass, Emma snapped one out of my fingers. I pointed out to her that it is rather 'rude behaviour' to snap the pass out of my hand. This comment, however, prompted her to say that I was aggressive towards her, and that the pilot should call the police to receive me at the airport. The pilot then joined the situation, and after a few explanations there was no more talk about the police.

- *Does OWA find such behaviour acceptable within its code of conduct for staff? Is it appropriate according to OWA to snatch things out of customers' hands? Is it according to OWA policy to threaten with police when a customer complains about rude staff behaviour?*
- *What protection does OWA offer to its customers from staff conduct? Do you have a 'zero tolerance' policy that applies to customers as well?*
- *What happens to the personal details collected by members of staff, such as passport details and booking reference? What legitimacy do staff have, especially with regard to passport details?*

The final situation was witnessed by my wife who describes it below. As we were leaving the plane, crew members were lined up and were thanking us [probably prescribed by company policy]. For the first time, after many years of travelling by plane, we did not feel like thanking anyone so we left quietly. Just behind me was the lady passenger involved in the initial incident. The crew members said 'thank you' to her and she replied 'I wish I could say the same'. The pilot then said to her 'I won't have you treating my staff like this' and physically pushed her out of the plane. I was shocked by his behaviour and all I could say was 'you pushed her, in front of me'. The lady was also shaken. I was holding my 9-month old baby in my arms and was too scared to get further involved as I was on top of the staircase.

- *Do you justify this behaviour from staff members, especially from the captain? And, once again, what policies are there to protect customers from such behaviour from staff?*

One would assume that even if the behaviour of the lady passenger was rude, that a trained professional would be able to deal with it in a composed and civilized manner. It was more than clear that this woman was not a threat to staff or passengers so it is very worrying that she was treated like this. One would expect particularly from the captain to be able to keep situations under control.

– *Does OWA provide staff training to ensure that staff behave appropriately to customers? Does this training deal with difficult situations and what guidance do you give to staff for such cases?*

To conclude, we travel as a family with two young children. We have spent last year alone in excess of xxxx for flights taken with OWA. We have been travelling for many years and have **never** witnessed such behaviour during a flight or in any other service setting for that matter. We left the plane saddened and intimidated. As parents, we want to ensure that we, and most importantly our children, travel in a **clean**, **safe** and **civilized**, **non-violent** environment and that we are **not threatened** as soon as we try to protect our rights. For this reason we request an official answer to our questions along with an apology.

Kind regards,
[The authors]

Index

Printed and bound by CPI Group (UK) Ltd, Croydon, CR0 4YY

24/04/2025

14661321-0001